God, Jesus
and
Belief

To Fiona, Kirsten and Duncan

God, Jesus and Belief

The Legacy of Theism

STEWART R. SUTHERLAND

Basil Blackwell

First published 1984
Basil Blackwell Publisher Limited
108 Cowley Road, Oxford OX4 1JF, England

Basil Blackwell Inc.
432 Park Avenue South, Suite 1505
New York, NY 10016, USA

British Library Cataloguing in Publication Data

Sutherland, Stewart
    God, Jesus and belief.
    1. God
    I. Title
    231 BT102

    ISBN 0–631–13548–0
    ISBN 0–631–13591–X Pbk

Typeset by Oxford Publishing Services, Oxford
Printed in Great Britain by The Camelot Press Ltd,
Southampton

Contents

Preface

My thanks are due to the Electors to the Wilde Lectureship in the University of Oxford for the invitation to deliver the Wilde Lectures in Oxford during the three academic years 1981–84. This book is based upon the first twelve lectures given in 1981 and 1982. The hospitality shown by many colleagues in Oxford was always generous and Basil Mitchell's courtesy as a chairman was matched only by his kindness as a host.

The preparation of the manuscript has been helped by the critical scrutiny given to sections of it by colleagues and post-graduates in seminar at King's College, London, and Miss Betty Wood typed the manuscript with characteristic care and patience.

Part I

God and Agnosticism

1

The Changing Face of Belief

What men and women believe about God varies greatly from one age and one culture to another. At some times and in some places, matters seem to settle down and a consensus emerges. Ours is not such an age. Radicalism and conservatism in religion pull vigorously in opposite directions. Superstition and 'scientism' are so intertwined in popular attitudes that the idea of a common ground of reasonable belief has almost died. Religious belief, which has internal coherence and undisputed congruences with the many other beliefs which make up the fabric of our lives, seems to be the dream of a past age of philosophical theologians.

Thus I cannot share the self-confidence implicit in for example, John Locke's hope that there is readily to hand a set of religious beliefs which, without much controversy, will command widespread or even universal assent:

> Since then the precepts of Natural Religion are plain, and very intelligible to all mankind, and seldom come to be controverted; and other revealed truths, which are conveyed to us by books and languages, are liable to the common and natural obscurities and difficulties incident to words: methinks it would become us more to be careful and diligent in observing the former and less magisterial, positive and imperious in imposing our own sense and interpretation of the latter.[1]

For all sorts of reasons which are not the immediate concern of this book, we can no longer think in these terms. This is not to capitulate to the intellectual *kamikaze* pilots who espouse a radical form of relativism, because of course the equation of the *truth* of a set of beliefs with the widespread *acknowledgement* of that truth is a mistake which belongs to the prejudices of the Enlightenment rather than of the twentieth century. Disagreement presupposes rather than excludes the idea of truth, but it does sometimes make progress towards truth exceptionally slow and painstaking. If there is progress in this book, then it will be evident that the first steps, and indeed the second, must be negative.

None the less, there are two immensely rich sources available to those in our culture who wish to confront seriously the central question of religious belief. The first is the strength and sophistication fo the Christian tradition within European thought and sensibility. To forestall the cry of 'parochialism' from the many who are properly concerned with the multiplicity of religions, may it suffice to say that one must start somewhere, and what is more sensible than to start from where 'we' are, which is as inheritors of European culture and the Christianity which has dominated it.

This leads to a second legacy of that culture – an ongoing and equally sophisticated awareness of the nature of reason and argument about matters religious as well as non-religious. An enquiry concerning what may be proposed for belief has then at least two means of plotting its progress: the one, the broad stream of Christian theism; the other, over two millenia of philosophical reflection on the nature and place of argument and reason. Unfortunately these two have often been disputative neighbours and it would be unreasonable to expect this to change overnight. The disputes, however, very often arise on the one hand from narrowness of interpretation of the Christian tradition, or on the other from unnecessarily restrictive accounts of what constitutes an argument or a piece of reasoning.

What is clear is that there is room for significant disagreement both about the Christian tradition and its place in European culture, and the nature of reasoning and its place in our culture, and it may be that my suggestion that we have two rich resources from which to start our enquiry appears simplistic or over-optimistic in its implications. I must correct such an impression.

There will be those who, having read this book, will regard as disingenuous my reference to the importance of the Christian tradition, for there is much that has been central to that tradition which I shall either discard, or leave on one side like an engine idling in a neutral gear with apparently no role to play in the affairs of life. I shall give reasons for all such claims, but inevitably it will often be a matter of judgement rather than proof. The only alternative would at times be complete suspense of judgement and that cannot be part of an acceptable strategy in such matters.

It is important to be clear about what is at stake here. My intention is not to restate *the* Christian message or theology for today, since such a formulation presupposes too much. Writers as varied as Locke and Rudolf Bultmann have believed implicitly that it is possible to restate Christian belief without altering its core or content. This is less excusable in Bultmann than in Locke, for Bultmann was the heir to rather than forerunner of the development of the awareness that Christianity in particular, and religion in general had a history. Bultmann's conclusion was that the essence or demythologized core of Christianity could somehow none the less be stated intact, having been preserved through the centuries, albeit in a radically different mythological form.

The mistake implicit in all this is to be found in the writings of many philosophers and theologians, for even those who do pay lip-service to the claim that Christianity is a historical religion, forget that this also implies that Christianity is a religion with a history which persists to the present day, and will in all likelihood continue into the future. We are the inheritors of Christianity *as it has developed over many centuries in many and various cultures*. As such, it is a tradition of immense richness which, if it is to survive, will have to continue to grow and develop. Each age imposes its own constraints and opportunities. My intention in this book is to identify some of the most central constraints now at work

and to give a picture of one possible, and, I believe, oppor-
tune development of this tradition. I must make clear at the
outset, however, that the method I am following implies
selectivity. Some elements of the tradition will play a new
and central part; others will, as our transatlantic colleagues so
aptly put it, be relegated to 'the back burner'; yet others may
to all intents and purposes be discarded completely. Such a
programme may imply foolhardiness, but it seems to me to
be no more, and no less, than what has been going on for the
past nineteen centuries. Indeed, it is a way of thinking possible only within a rich and developing tradition. In terms
used by Peter Strawson elsewhere, my purpose is, unlike
Strawson's essay in metaphysics, *revisionary* rather than
descriptive. This distinguishes my enterprise from three
different types of intellectual effort.

There are those who see their task as translating or inter-
preting a given deposit for today. This group includes such
strange bedfellows as Karl Barth and Bultmann, for in practice both assume that there is a clear essence or core in
Christianity and that the theologian's task is to re-present
that in either (Barth) less misleading or (Bultmann) less anti-
quated terms. One variation within this heading is to be
found amongst those philosophers who work avowedly and
confessionally within a picture of the Christian tradition,
such that if a conclusion does not fit with their account of the
'agreed' content of that tradition it would be unacceptable or
at least suspect. Thus, without necessarily wishing to endorse
R. B. Braithwaite's view on the nature of religious belief, or
more recently John Hick's account of a 'global theology', I
cannot accept, as a reason for rejecting their views, the fact
that these views are clearly *not* those of most Christians
throughout the ages, or most Christian theologians today.
Equally, I have reservations about endorsing the strategy of
the following argument by Peter Geach: 'And if someone says
that God's eternity is something simply out of relation with
what occurs in time – that we ought not to say e.g. that God
lived *before* the world came into existence – then his view is
probably confused and certainly unscriptural.'[2] If a view is

confused, it must be clarified; if a view is unscriptural, it may be none the worse for that.

Of course, it is reasonable to point out that a view is 'unscriptural', or that it is not what most Christians believe, or that it is not what Christianity 'essentially' is, if the view is being presented as falling under one of these descriptions. For example, much stimulus to the philosophical discussion of religious belief is to be found in the writing of D. Z. Phillips, but equally much sterile debate has resulted because both Phillips and his opponents have at times argued as if one appropriate criterion of the acceptability of his accounts of, say, petitionary prayer or the belief in external life, is whether or not this is what Christians *really* believe. Phillips has given weight to this by his interpretation and application of Wittgenstein's dictum that 'philosophy leaves everything as it is'. This is not the place for a full discussion of Phillips's views. It suffices to define my own enterprise over against his (and his opponents') by pointing out that I welcome his accounts of petitionary prayer and the belief in eternal life; *but* I welcome them as interesting constructions upon or revisions of the Christian tradition rather than as they are apparently offered, descriptions of the most essential or continuing elements of that tradition. It is not clear that Phillips would accept my emphasis on the terms 'construction' or 'revision'.

It is as well at this stage to bring into the picture the ever-present spectre of reductionism. There have been many attempts to give an account of religious belief which has purported to be descriptive but which has in the end been reductionist in emphasis. Many theologians have accused Phillips of this, but in so doing they have, I think, been mistaken. Of course some accounts have been deliberately and polemically reductionist – for example Feuerbach's *The Essence of Christianity* – and others, including Braithwaite's, have in fact turned out to be reductionist whether or not this was the original intention.

Now I do think that the issue of reductionism is very important, but I do also believe that it is often a distraction

from more important questions. Its distractive capacities
derive from a tactic in argument often used by those anti-
pathetic to religion, and it is an intellectual sleight of hand
which ought to be exposed for what it is. The tactic is to ask
religious believers what meaning 'in plain terms' they attach
to expressions which are typical and distinctive of religious
language. If the response appears to be adequate, and an
account of the meaning of such terms as 'God' or 'salvation'
or 'miracle' is given in 'plain terms', then the counter takes
the form of 'Ah! You mean by "God" or "salvation" nothing
more than . . . But that is reductionism. "Salvation" now
means no more than "total well-being" . . .', and so on.

If, however, the response is sufficiently careful to avoid
such an interpretation, then the counter is the charge of
'fideism', for there does seem to be some element of the
meaning of these expressions which is opaque to the philosopher who wants a translation 'in plain terms'. There are
many subtle and sophisticated forms of this intellectual pin-
cer movement, but much of the argument in recent philosophy of religion has been of this form in one way or another.
In so far as it has , the discussion of reductionism has been a
distraction.

The important issue raised by the charge of reductionism is
whether the language of religion is simply an inflated and
metaphorical way of saying what can more clearly and easily
be said otherwise. Any such reductionist account of religion,
if legitimate, would lead to very important intellectual conclusions about religious belief, as Feuerbach, for example,
and Marx after him, were well aware. Conversely, if a reductionist account of religion is in error, it is important to devise
a means of establishing this. The problems facing philosophers of religion here, and the tactics used by some, are not
unique to religion. For example, the President of the Law
Society of Scotland for 1980–81, Michael Park, faced a parallel dilemma in his pioneering attempts to make the law more
accessible and intelligible to the layman. He discovered that
on occasions when there were not obvious translations of
legal terms into non-specialist language, he was faced with

the standard criticism of legal procedures being 'deliberately secretive'. Whatever case there is for pointing out that some lawyers may conceive it to be in their interest to be to some extent secretive, I have no doubt of the strength of the point which Park has made in reply: 'The plain fact is there are as many legal terms as there are engineering terms which mean nothing to the man in the street, but which mean a great deal to a lawyer or an engineer. It is simply not possible in my view to reduce all legal terminology and phraseology to simple words.'[3] The parallels are quite striking, even down to the charge of a form of 'fideism'.

The parallel can be pursued further, however, for the legal case can help us see that there is a way of avoiding the painful dilemma offered by the two-pronged fork of either reductionism or fideism/secretiveness. On the one hand there is no barrier in principle to anyone who wishes obtaining access to the appropriate sources, and thereby coming to understand for himself how the legal language operates and what the various terms mean. The same is true in the case of religion. An apocryphal story is told of T. S. Eliot, faced by an interviewer's criticism that many who had atempted to read his poetry had not understood it because of the many classical allusions in it: according to the story Eliot's uncompromising reply was, 'Well, they will damn well have to learn, won't they?' The case is not completely parallel, but the general point stands: the fact that something is not translatable into 'plain terms' does not thereby in principle make the understanding of it impossible.

To revert to Park's statement on legal language, a second useful pointer is found in the supporting comment of Professor Phillip Love that 'Any attempt to simplify legal language would probably require a large number of court actions simply to determine what the new language meant.' (ibid.) There are two important points here. The first is that particular languages – whether constituting the legal tradition of Scotland or the theistic tradition of Christianity – have work to do. If they are still 'living', they perform these tasks because they are as they are. (I shall not here pursue the implications of this for a Bultmannian outlook.) If, further, one succumbs to the pressure to translate the language of religion into 'plain terms', then in all probability the 'new' language will fail to do the job which is expected of it. However, for this to be acceptable as an argument against reductionist procedures, it will have to be established that there is a task for the language of theism to which it is peculiarly, or possibly even uniquely, fitted. I shall return to the question of uniqueness in due course. The second point is that if one does go through the process of substituting different or 'simpler' words for the words characteristic of religious belief, the problem is by no means resolved. For example in the teachings of Jesus in the fourth gospel a great deal hangs on the shifts in nuance and even meaning given to the *prima facie* 'simple' or 'straightforward' terms used to carry religious sense. For example the uses of the terms 'clean', 'peace', 'servant', 'master', 'know' and 'hear' in the 'Farewell Discourses' of John 13 and 14, depend upon contrasting the 'plain' with the 'religious' sense. The court actions required within law to clarify the meaning of the 'new language' will be no help here, but undoubtedly the terms 'clean', 'peace', 'know' and so on are not being used univocally throughout these discourses. This is precisely the point of the following interchange: '"If you know me you would know my Father too. From now on you do know him; you have seen him." Philip said to him, "Lord, show us the Father and we ask no more".' A rather pedantic, but for the moment perhaps a helpful way of putting the point, is that Philip has yet to learn that the 'plain' or 'simple' words 'know' and 'see' mean more in this context than at first appears.

Of course a sceptic will hint at obfuscation, secretiveness or fideism, and I do accept that these are gravitational pulls against which religion must always struggle. The counter-weights will be the attempt to identify clearly the distinctive tasks of the language of theism, and the careful plotting of the path of understanding in such a way as to rule out any appeal to initiation rites rather than learning, or to forms of special pleading rather than reasoned statement.

The nature of the enquiry excludes all such devices. There will be no appeal to 'truths' which are revealed only to initiates. Thus any claim whose truth can be supported by appeal *only* to an authoritative source outside of the community of argument and discussion, cannot be given special status or consideration. This applies to alleged revealed truths, whether they are to be found in books, in the *ex cathedra* pronouncements of individuals, or somehow mysteriously buried in a 'tradition'; or whether again, more fashionably for the moment, they are hidden, like the gold at the end of the rainbow, at the conclusion of a long process of initiation and submission. Now I am not denying that as a matter of psychology and biography each of the above might provide the *occasion* of learning, but I am rejecting the view that argues that this occasion is *necessary* and *exclusive*. There are two elements to this: in the first place I am denying that a necessary condition of coming to believe what is true can be the acceptance of the authority of *this* person or *this* book or *this* initiation, although as a matter of fact some may come to truth in this way. However to claim legitimately that what one believes is the truth, it is not enough to say that it is commended by a particular authoritative source. In the second place I am rejecting the idea of truths whose sense is only discernible by those who accept them. Unbelievers may sometimes reject belief because they have no understanding, but clearly there are also unbelievers who know exactly what they are refusing to assent to when they reject religious belief.

This brings us to a brief consideration of the second great legacy of our culture – the tradition of argument and reflection upon the nature of reason and reasoning. The account which we are prepared to give of the scope and nature of reasons and reasoning is important for all areas of life. It is crucial that we do not allow ourselves to be confined within an over-narrow understanding of reason and argument. Thus in excluding certain sorts of appeal to authority as providing 'foundations' for religious belief, I do not propose to replace these by a better or stronger 'foundation'.

Philosophers and theologians have sometimes attempted to locate such alternative foundations in some pattern of reasoning. The result of this has often been to constrain philosophical discussion within the strait-jacket of, for example, a Humean picture of reasoning which consigned and confined the use of reason to one of two areas – 'relations of ideas' or 'matters of fact'. Interestingly, none of Hume's major philosophical conclusions depended upon such 'foundations', although his writings are full of reasoning.

There are two points I wish to make here. The first is that I am not basing what follows upon a 'foundationalist' view of epistemology, which would demand a rigid structuring of beliefs into a hierarchical order where the truth of all rests ultimately upon the truth of a few which are somehow self-validating or self-authenticated. The difficulties of such a view have been explored in great detail by many contemporary philosophers, including for example Quine, and most recently Richard Rorty. However, alternatives to foundationalism are not recent innovations, for philosophers as diverse as Socrates and Kant have defined and practised radically different forms of 'non-foundational' philosophical enquiry.

The second point focuses on the terms 'reason' and 'reasonable'. As John Wisdom so often elegantly demonstrated, there are many examples of philosophical reasoning which do not fit into the moulds of inductive and deductive arguments. This is not the place to survey what Wisdom, or Socrates for that matter, show us about the nature of philosophical argument and, by implication, about the nature of rational discussion; but particularly important for our purpose is Wisdom's stress upon the variety of ways in which someone can be persuaded of a truth by coming to see that truth in a new light. There is an affinity here with the parables of Jesus. One clear example of an attempt to persuade another of a truth of the greatest importance is to be found in the section of the tenth chapter of St Luke's gospel which begins with the lawyer's question. 'Master, what shall

I do to inherit eternal life?', and ends with Jesus's counter-question, 'Which now of these three, thinkest thou, was neighbour unto him that fell among thieves?' The discussion which leads to the telling of the story of the good Samaritan is certainly neither irrational nor a-rational, but it is an attempt to persuade rather than indoctrinate – that is to say, it has to do with the statement and reasonable defence of a belief which if true is of ultimate significance. But that defence cannot be analysed into patterns of argument which are either inductive or deductive in structure.

There are immense dangers in allowing our picture of what counts as reasonable and unreasonable, or of the nature of argument and persuasion, to become obsessively narrow. Later chapters will explore more fully some examples of the range of reasonable and persuasive argument about religious beliefs. For the moment it suffices to have given an indication of what is to be regarded as the alternative to 'revealed' – in the sense of 'exclusive' – truths, namely conclusions based on rational discussion which if not already, in Locke's terms, 'plain' to all mankind, must at least in principle be 'intelligible' to them. I have not dared to entertain the hope of not being controverted; I do intend to offer views which are at least in principle possible to controvert, for affirmations will be made and defended by arguments which are meant to persuade.

The outcome of the application of the above guidelines is presented in the next twelve chapters. The conclusions relate quite clearly to the three sections of the book. This first section is largely negative in its conclusions. It is an exposition of the unease felt by many in talking of God as a person, or as an entity or individual. There are I believe severe difficulties in giving an adequate account of such talk, and these are summarized in chapter 4. However, even if one could, the implications of such a theology are to make the problems of evil and suffering even more intractable than they appear at first sight. My approach to these matters is outlined in chapter 2. The positive point which I wish to propose in all this is the importance of ethical considerations in the construction of a theology or in outlining an acceptable *credo*. It is this, I believe, which relieves what might appear to be a bleak negative path to agnosticism, and the discussion of chapter 3 is quite central to the view which I go on to outline in the second section of the book.

This section is concerned to answer the question of what remains if one does find oneself unable to confess belief in a personal God. Essentially my answer is that theism has been the vehicle in Western thinking which has most consistently given expression to the possibility of a view of human affairs which is not the view of any one individual or group of individuals, i.e. a view of human affairs *sub specie aeternitatis*. Whether there is, in principle, such a view is the most important religious and perhaps philosophical question which can be posed. The exposition of this claim is offered in chapters 6 and 7. A condition of the argument of these chapters is a particular view of the nature of theology – 'the articulation of the possible' – and this is outlined in chapter 5. The last chapter of this section relates this to discussion of the realization of this in the lives of individuals and prepares the way for the final section.

In chapters 9 to 12 I engage with issues which on the whole philosophers of religion have been inclined to avoid or neglect. Perhaps there is foolhardiness here, but it does seem to me odd and indeed unsatisfactory that philosophers of religion who have discussed in great depth aspects of Christian theism have not been willing to reflect on the implications of their views for what one makes of the founder of that religion. Inevitably there is the risk of the amateur impinging on specialist fields, but these matters are too important to be left to specialists alone. In addition there are, as I hope these chapters demonstrate, some crucial philosophical questions which affect quite directly what may or may not be said about the figure of Jesus. In part my argument is that the account of the nature of transcendence which I have outlined will help clarify both these questions and the possible answers to them.

Of course anyone may outline a *credo*, but is it not a

mistake to suppose that it should have more than personal significance? The first point to be made is that what is offered is offered as more than an account of the author's state of mind. What is proposed is a system of belief which is undoubtedly in certain respects Christian, although equally certainly it is in other respects deeply heterodox. The line between the two, however, is not drawn arbitrarily, for it is a response to intellectual pressures and provocations which are part of the inheritance which is ours. I do not wish to say that this is what all *must* reasonably believe, but I do suggest both that it is believable and that it draws significantly on the Christian tradition. The problem for any reader is of course one of deciding on what ground some might reject or possibly even accept such a proposed system of belief. There will be those who reject it because it is unorthodox. So be it, but what then do they make of chapters 2 and 4?

To help those who look for rather different grounds of assessment, I wish to propose certain criteria for the assessment of any proposed system of belief. These are not sufficient criteria, but in the case of the third, fourth and fifth I believe that they are necessary conditions of the accceptability of a system of religious belief. The first two criteria I am stipulating as necessary: perhaps they are part of my *credo*.

These first two criteria are echoes of writings of previous generations, to which this work might be regarded as a modest footnote – Schleiermacher's *On Religion: Speeches to its Cultured Despisers*, and Kant's *Religion Within the Limits of Reason Alone*. Whatever the intention in each case, the outcome was a revisionary account of religious belief.

CRITERION 1 *Any successful revision of the content of religious belief must be undertaken in the context of European culture as a whole.*

This is true whether or not we share Schleiermacher's qualms about the effects of that culture:

> Suavity and sociability, art and science have so fully taken possession of your minds, that no room remains for the eternal and holy Being that lies beyond the world. I know

how well you have succeeded in making your earthly life so rich and varied, that you no longer stand in need of an eternity.

The history of Christianity is shot through with the colourings of culture more broadly conceived, and vice-versa. Those who talk easily of the role of the tradition within theological reflection too often ignore this. The tradition was not formed and preserved within exclusive walls of orthodoxy: it belongs to and shapes and is shaped by the intellectual and spiritual questions which dominate European culture. A successful piece of revisionary work, as Schleiermacher clearly saw, will take account of the central questions posed by our culture to Christianity, and in so doing interrogate the presuppositions of that culture. Less prophetically, may it suffice to say that revisionary work must start where we are, which is as inheritors of European culture and the Christianity which has grown up within it.

CRITERION 2   A religious belief which runs counter to our moral beliefs is to that extent unacceptable.

Very often lip-service is paid to this view, but when difficulties arise, there is a retreat to the self-indulgent intellectual comfort of talk of 'mystery' and 'inscrutability'. Less often, but more strikingly, the gauntlet to moral belief is thrown down, and we are reminded of our status as finite creatures who have to live with paradox in one form or another. Kierkegaard's Fear and Trembling is the classic and awful example of this. Each of these two ways of modifying this second criterion will be examined in due course. In the meantime may I provocatively affirm Kant's general principle, if not detailed conclusions, about the priority of moral beliefs over religious ones?

CRITERION 3   The acceptability of a form of religious belief is related to its comprehensiveness in the sense which it makes of our experience of the world in which we find ourselves.

This is a criterion which applies not only to our present experience and our communal and individual histories, but also to possible future experience. Religions have died because of their inability to cope with changing historical circumstances. One of the great strengths of Christianity has been its capacity and resourcefulness in coping with change. This is not to argue that all change must be 'accommodated' within a religious outlook, but rather that changes to which no response – whether of rejection of modification or accept-ance – is offered are changes which are 'not dreamt of in that philosophy' and which therefore define the limitations of the outlook in question. Thus whether Christianity can offer to its adherents a means of defining their relation to, for example, the changing views of life and death arising from developments in genetics, is a crucial question about the viability of Christianity in the years to come. Equally a religion found to be systematically ignoring or denying cer-tain truths about human beings, or the world in which they live, is to that extent vulnerable.

CRITERION 4   A revisionary account of religious belief both commends itself and avoids the dangers of reductionism to the extent to which it gives or preserves insights which are not available elsewhere, into the human condition, or into the world in which we live.

This criterion is immensely important and will be discus-sed in detail in due course. The implications of this point were raised by R. W. Hepburn when he discussed the following proposition: 'If we *were* to abandon all talk of "God" . . . we should immediately cease to be able to make sense of many things which that concept *does* make sense of.'[4] In *The Sovereignty of Good*[5] Iris Murdoch has explored some of these questiosn as they arise in the context of moral philos-ophy. It is important to stress that what is being discussed here is not whether as a contingent matter of fact individuals who believe X have insights which others do not have. Quite the contrary. The issue is about the limits of our thinking and seeing and feeling which are as a matter of logic set by the language or system or beliefs with which we are operating. Stuart Hampshire, whose *Thought and Action*[6] repays careful study in this context, offers the following relevant comments: '. . . the habits and rules of my thinking limit the possibilities of action for me . . . The limits of a man's habits of thought are limits also of what he can be expected to try to do . . .'

The reason for this, I should argue, is that the motives and emotions which in the end move us to action depend upon the availability of a whole range of descriptions of ourselves, of others and of the world. Thus I cannot be moved to discover God's will for me or for my community, if the conception of the will of God does not belong to my way of talking and thinking. A genuine (i.e. non-reductionist) religious belief will add to that stock of descriptions. This is one very important criterion to which a revisionary account of religious belief might appeal in trying to gain acceptance.

CRITERION 5   *A revisionary account of religious belief is acceptable to the extent to which it makes and defends a claim to be true.*

2

God and Evil:
Starting All Over Again

> But as to saying that God, who is good, becomes the cause of
> evil to anyone, we must contend in every way that neither
> should anyone assert this in his own city if it is to be well
> governed, nor anyone hear it . . .[1]

Whatever we may care to say of Plato's view of literary
censorship, there can be little doubt of his theological insight
on this point. Evil cannot be ascribed to a God who is good
and in the end this is the force of my second criterion of the
adequacy of an account of religious belief – 'a religious belief
which runs counter to our moral beliefs is to that extent
unacceptable.' The problems raised by the presence of evil on
our earth and suffering in our experience are the most daunting and profound to face the theist. If we are to follow Plato's
injunction – and what else can we do if we are to avoid
changing the meaning of the word 'good' when applied to
God? – then what are we to make of the fact that this world
knows evil and is acquainted with suffering? Many answers
to that question have been devised, of which the intellectually
most economic and, for some, the spiritually least destructive, is Plato's:

> God desired that all things should be good and nothing bad,
> *so far as this was attainable.* (my italics)[2]

> . . . the creation of this world is the combined work of necessity and mind. Mind, the ruling power, persuaded necessity to bring *the greater part of* created things to perfection and thus and after this manner in the beginning, through necessity made subject to reason, this universe was created. (my italics)[3]

But of course this picture of limitation is a diminution not of the idea of goodness, but of the idea of God.

This is according to the classic outline of the problem and very often it takes the form of an either/or: either we must renounce absolute claim to the goodness of God or we will impute limitation to him in respect of power or knowledge. For, it is argued, if we do not accept one of these alternatives, then we shall be forced to deny the reality of evil and suffering.

My intention is not to summarize and rehearse all that has been written by philosophers and theologians about evil and suffering, although some reference to this will be necessary. Initially, however, I wish to comment upon the location of the problem within the structure of theology. My proposal is for a theology which *begins* with the problem of evil and suffering, for I believe that such a beginning would produce a theology radically different from most intellectual schemes which go under that heading. If we are to follow Locke's suggestion of looking for what is 'plain' and starting there, we would do well to start with evil and suffering. In terms of the difficulty which it may pose for the theologian we might prefer to start elsewhere, but in terms of what is plain and incontrovertible the fact of suffering has rather more than an edge on Calvin's insistence that we *begin* with an account of the knowledge of God, or Tillich's emphasis upon 'the structure of reason', or Barth's on the relationship between theology and the Church

Now my admiration for the *grandeur* of the theological enterprises represented respectively by these three men is second to none. Nor would I deny the importance and sophistication of the questions which they pose and of the answers which they beat out on the anvil of European thought and sensibility. In each case, however, the direction of the discussion is to make what we say about suffering dependent upon and compatible with an already elaborated theological and religious outlook. My intention is to reverse the direction of the discussion, to begin with the plain fact of suffering, and to see what can be said theologically and religiously that is compatable with such a beginning. Thus my present concern is most definitely not theodicy, for I do not believe that theodicy – the justification of the ways of God to man – is possible. My reasons for this will become apparent in due course. However, I am not proposing as an alternative a form of linear enquiry in which the sole criterion and sole justification of what may be said theologically is to be found in the contemplation of suffering and evil. What is being outlined is one starting point and one criterion of what is acceptable. The starting point – the fact of suffering – may strike some as novel, but it can hardly be said to be peripheral to the Christian tradition. The criterion – that all that is said of God must not define his goodness in such a way that it requires us to subdue or abandon fundamental moral beliefs – is perhaps more open to debate. That it should be is itself a point of great interest, and one which will be explored further.

There will emerge from this stage of the enquiry some tentative and, I must admit, apparently negative or limiting conclusions. One qualification of and two comments on this point must be offered: the qualification is that I hope to demonstrate to you that the sense of loss or constriction is only apparent, but that the path to that point of agreement descends through several circles before we may safely turn upwards again. The first comment is that the interim conclusions here will be confirmed by appeal to issues other than our starting point of suffering and the goodness of God: the second comment is that to start from the presence of evil and suffering is not *ipso facto* to adopt a standpoint which is literally 'woeful' and pessimistic. That human beings are capable of suffering is not, thank God, the only universal truth about the human condition. Further elaboration of this is postponed rather than precluded.

As we have already reminded ourselves, the standard form of the discussion of evil and suffering is that of theodicy and its antithesis. In order to show why I find this form of the discussion unsuitable for my purposes, I must first outline its contours. On the one hand there are those who would point to the facts of suffering and evil in order to raise doubts in the believer's mind about the many claims made of the God of monotheism – that he is omnipotent, omniscient, good and loving. On the other, there are those who reply by arguing that apparent incompatibilities in what is believed of God are indeed only apparent.

Between the contemporary antagonists there seems to be one point of agreement: that no formal contradiction can be derived from the three propositions:

(1) God is omnipotent and omniscient;
(2) God is completely good;
(3) the world contains instances of evil and suffering.

For as Mackie, Mitchell and Holland all agree,[4] at least one further premise must be added if an inconsistency is to be established. On the one side Mackie insists upon the inclusion of a step in the argument to show that 'a good omnipotent thing eliminates evil completely', and on the other Mitchell insists that it must be *established* rather than assumed that there could not be 'morally sufficient reasons for God's permitting evil'. In each case what is being assumed is that it is appropriate to discuss evil and suffering as a *problem for and constituted by* a pre-formed theology. Some theists point out forcibly that the 'problem of evil' depends upon belief in a God of a certain kind for its very formulation. This is tantamount to identifying 'the problem of evil' with theodicy, and the natural consequence is that the debate focuses upon God's motives, intentions, 'sufficient reasons' (Mitchell) or self-consistency (Mackie).

It is, I believe, pedantic to point out to a Camus or a Dostoevsky that the rebel who is outraged by a moral order which so tolerates undeserved and 'pointless' suffering is not thinking clearly. Surely one does not have to be, or to have

been, a monotheist to be appalled and angered by the suffering which some undergo? There are two ways of supporting
this point. First there is nothing odd or inconsistent in the
distress which someone might feel at the imbalance between
one's recognized moral obligations and the principles of fair-
ness and justice embedded in them, and the evident breaches
of these same moral principles in the dispositions of providence. Such is the essence of moral outrage evoked by the
misfortunes of others. Indeed far from requiring monotheis-
tic beliefs to make the sense of such a discrepancy intelligible,
Kant used the sense of such imbalance *in order to state* a case
for theism.

The second support for my initial claim is to be found in
the fact that even if an intellectual solution were available for
the problems posed to the theist by evil and suffering, we
might still have *moral* difficulty in wholeheartedly assenting
to such a 'solution'. Suppose we were to find 'a morally
sufficient reason' for God's permission of the realities of evil
and suffering as we know them, would that be the end of it?
Would we be satisfied? One does not have to be an Ivan
Karamazov to have qualms about that. Perhaps the human
analogy which gives clearest definition to the dilemma to
which I point is to be found in the affairs of statecraft and
particularly those murky areas of them in which apparent
evils are permitted for 'morally sufficient reasons'. This area
of human sensibility is charted with elegance and insight by
John Le Carré in his most recent novels. The growth of
complexity in the character of George Smiley is an achievement of real distinction, and is an unusually apt illustration of
the point I am making. Whatever the personal complications
of his dealings with master-spy Karla of the KGB, Smiley
had morally sufficient reason to view the aim of Karla's
enforced defection to the West as a duty. Yet note the
ambiguity of his reaction when, as recounted in *Smiley's
People*, he completes successfully, and humanely, the interro-
gation which will lead to this:

> And Smiley, sitting so quiet, so immobile, as the party broke
> up around him, what did he feel? On the face of it this was a

moment of high achievement for him. He had done everything he had set out to do, and more, *even if he had resorted to
Karla's techniques for the purpose*. He had done it alone; and
today as the record would show he had broken and turned
Karla's handpicked agent in the space of a couple of hours.
Unaided, even hampered by those who had called him back
to service, he had fought his way through to the point where
he could honestly say he had burst the last important lock. He
was in late age, yet his tradecraft had never been better; for
the first time in his career, he held the advantage over his old
adversary.

On the other hand, that adversary had acquired a human
face of disconcerting clarity. It was no brute whom Smiley
was pursuing with such mastery, no unqualified fanatic after
all, no automaton. It was a man; and one whose downfall, if
Smiley chose to bring it about, would be caused by nothing
more sinister than excessive love, a weakness with which
Smiley himself from his own tangled life was eminently
familiar. (my italics)[5]

Morally sufficient reasons for the permission of evil and
suffering may seem convincing in the abstract. The human
face of the victim belongs to a different dimension. It is
difficult to see how one might be persuaded then, and it
would be wrong to be persuaded now, that from the
eschatological standpoint of eternity there is a morally
sufficient reason adequate to remove the uncertainties and
ambiguities of moral sentiment so well portrayed by Le
Carré in such a different context. The point is that even a
convinced and loyal subject, even a convinced and believing
theist, may well recognize that the moral sentiments are not
at the beck and call of intellectual consistency. That can be a
strength, as well as a weakness.

Some theodicists will have none of this and would heartily
ban such 'false' sentiment in the name of rationality. They
speculate happily about the motives of their God and also
about the good reason which he might have for permitting
states of affairs which might appal lesser beings. For
example, the skill and sophistication of Richard Swinburne's
account of the arguments for the existence of God seem to

lapse in his account of the presumably 'morally' sufficient reason which God might have for apparently giving different instructions to the opposing armies surrounding Jerusalem at the time of the Crusades:

> Thus a Muslim may have an experience of being told by God to defend Jerusalem against the infidel, while a Christian has the experience of being told by God to attack it. This might be explained by the fact that in the course of human history as a result of factors for which men are to blame. Muslims and Christians have come to different and very limited understandings of God. God is very anxious that human understanding of God should develop through human experience, effort, and co-operation, and should not always be revealed by divine intervention, yet he is also very anxious that at any time in history men should live and die by the ideals which they then have. He therefore tells Muslim and Christian each to live by their current ideals; knowing that the experience of so doing may lead them into a deeper understanding.[6]

Well! I should be prepared to swap one hint of Smiley's uncertainty for volumes of such assurance about the acceptability of the motives and reasons of such a God. In fact Swinburne's remarks here exemplify in frightening clarity what I mean when I point to the dangers of attempting to fit one's view of evil and suffering to a preframed theology. The word most apt here is 'Procrustean': '*Procrustean*, a. Tending to produce uniformity by violent methods (f. Gk. *Prokroustes*, Lit. stretcher, name of a fabulous robber who fitted victims to his bed by stretching or mutilation, *Concise Oxford Dictionary*).'

There are many, however, who are not thus 'Procrustean'. For example, Basil Mitchell shows a sensitive awareness of just the point at issue in his double insistence that '. . . although the existence and character of evil cannot be shown to be strictly incompatible with the creation of the world by an omnipotent and loving God, it does torture the faith of the believer more than any other circumstance . . .'.[7] Where I differ from Mitchell, however, is over the addition which he then makes of the words '. . . and demands a theodicy'. If the torture of which he speaks is moral in character, then, as in the case of Smiley, even a theodicy which consists of 'morally sufficient reasons' will not be adequate for complete peace of mind.

The profundity of these issues is daunting and this is doubtless part of the reason for the recurrence of terms such as 'mystery' and 'incomprehensibility' in discussions of evil and suffering. Since the appeal to these expressions can take a variety of forms – some intellectually less reputable than others – it will prove instructive to examine in detail one or two cases where the dangers of superficiality are avoided.

In his classic *Evil and the God of Love*, John Hick stresses both the mystery and incomprehensibility of evil, but also continues to argue that one need not be purely defensive here. 'Our "solution", then, to this baffling problem of excessive and undeserved suffering is a frank appeal to the positive value of mystery . . . "Thus, paradoxically", as H.H. Farmer says, "the failure of theism to solve all mysteries becomes part of its case!"'[8] On this view the mystery of evil and suffering is understood as contributing towards what Hick identifies as 'the Irenaean strand of Christian thought', in so far as it is one element of what makes this world a vale of soul-making. It is interesting to contrast what Hick suggests here with one of the major strands in Plato's thought. Whereas Hick implies that our not understanding certain things of ultimate significance is, to put it crudely, 'good for us', Plato identified virtue with knowledge and regarded ignorance, even at this deep level, as a hindrance to moral growth.

My intention here is not to provoke a confrontation of one view with the other, but rather to note how such a divergence arises. In Plato's case there is a clear connection between his identification of knowledge and virtue and his account of the presence of evil in this world. 'So far as this was attainable' God desired all things to be good. There is no mystery here of the sort indicated by Hick. We are not left with *moral* doubts about the goodness of God: nor do we have the problem of trying vainly to comprehend how God could have 'morally sufficient reasons' to licence the degree of evil and suffering which we see around us. Of course, theologically the cost is high, and I shall return to this point, but first let us consider how the need to insist on mystery develops in Professor Hick's case.

In the end the reason is that Hick takes an established theology to the problem of evil. The established theology, in rudiments, consists of the first two of the three propositions listed earlier in this chapter concerning God's omnipotence and omniscience and his goodness. I stress again that I am here being descriptive rather than evaluative and am simply pointing to one of the elements which leads to talk of 'mystery' and 'incomprehensibility'. These terms arise because of the nature of, and priority given to, a particular and to some extent detailed definition of God. Such a definition drives us, in the face of evil, to the dual expedients of looking for 'morally sufficient reasons' and also underwriting the need for giving a central place *in this context* to mystery. It might be argued that in the central books of the *Republic* – in the use he makes of the similes of the Sun and the Line – Plato admits the importance of at least mystical vision of some sort. This is true, but irrelevant. The difference is that Hick's reference to mystery is to what is incomprehensible, whereas Plato's reference to a mystical insights is to a means of comprehension appropriate to its object. In the end, Hick believes that recognition of the fact that we are ignorant, that we cannot understand, can both be good for us morally and also be the basis of a theodicy. I would accept the first of these two points, but not the second. The central point, however, is that he is led to construe our lack of comprehension in this way *because of what he believes that we know about God*.

The same tendency is to be seen at work even more explicitly in the writing of Mitchell and Hans Kung. Mitchell is very circumspect in what he writes, and in *The Justification of Religious Belief* he limits his comments to the following: '. . . the Christian claims that, if the scheme is as he believes it to be, there is an irreducible element of mystery in it, and he would not expect, here and now, to be able to fit everything in' (p. 44). The spirit of St Paul's 'through a glass darkly' is to be applauded, but I would enter two *caveats*. In the first place there is a distinction to be drawn between what brings intellectual puzzlement – say an adequate account of the nature of God's relation to time, or of the doctrine of the incarnation – and what gives rise to moral uncertainty or even confusion. Thus whereas Plato may leave us in some puzzlement about the relation between mind and necessity, he quite firmly and rightly rejected any account of creation and providence which would give rise to moral misunderstanding. In the second place, whereas Mitchell's account might accord well with the traditional theism which moves from a roughly settled account of the belief in God to discussion of evil and suffering, it will not accord with the approach of natural religion being developed in this book. The nub of the disagreement is this: if we are to invoke the ideas of mystery and incomprehensibility at all, by what criteria do we decide when to appeal to them? There is something unacceptable about the tendency to invoke them in response to the questions raised by evil and suffering while apparently finding less difficulty in the *intellectually* equally problematic questions of the nature of God.

Mitchell is very cautious about this and it would be unfair to press my charge too firmly in his direction. I do believe that the question can still be legitimately addressed to him and to Hick, but Kung illustrates my main thesis there very clearly indeed and it is to two of his most recent books that I now turn. His general view is most clearly stated in *On Being a Christian*:

> Certainly it is possible to say that we cannot believe in God when we see the immense suffering of the world. But can this not be reversed? It is only if there is a God that we can look at all at this immense suffering in the world. *It is only in trusting faith in the incomprehensible*, always greater God that man can stride in justifiable hope through that broad, deep river: conscious of the fact that a hand is stretched out to him across the dark gulf of suffering and evil. (my italics)[9]

There is an ambiguity here as to whether it is God or suffering that is incomprehensible, and in one sense Kung's treatment of these issues in *Does God Exist?* does not resolve the problem. In this book he stresses 'Jesus' practical answer to the question of theodicy'. 'So far', it might be said, 'so good', for he apparently shares my qualms about theodicy. He writes,

> This is not a God at an ominous, transcendent distance, but close in incomprehensible goodness; he is a God who does not make empty promises about the hereafter or minimize the present darkness, futility and meaninglessness. Instead, in darkness, futility and meaninglessness, he invites us to the venture of hope.[10]

These words satisfy in spirit much of the emphasis of my second criterion of the adequacy of an account of religious belief. I shall in fact place much emphasis upon 'hope', but my analysis of this in chapter 12 will differ from that of Kung.

Despite this apparent point of contact, however, there are deep seated differences and these are made most apparent if I quote the two sentences which precede these remarks: Jesus' answer to the problems of evil and suffering point, Kung tells us, to 'God as Father':

> God as the Father who in his active providence and solicitude looks after every sparrow and every hair, who knows our needs before we ask him, makes our worries seem superfluous; God as the Father who knows everything in this far from perfect world and without whom nothing happens, whom man can absolutely trust and on whom he can completely rely even in suffering injustice, sin and death.

Now I find this quite extraordinary, and a lesser theologian than Kung might easily have to face a charge of being carried away by a pious sentimentality.

To begin with, the stress on this as a 'practical' as distinct from 'philosophical or theological justification of God' might seem a little disingenuous, for the above remarks contain, in other words, elements of the doctrines of God's omniscience, omnipotence and providential ordering of events. Further, remarks of the above type create rather than resolve (albeit 'practically') the problem of evil, for the presence of suffering and evil calls into question rather than is answered by the talk of sparrows and hair! It is precisely because traditional theism affirms that God 'knows everything' and that without him 'nothing happens', that the whole issue of evil and 'morally sufficient reasons' is quite as pressing as it is. What distinguishes a 'practical' solution from other theodicies is not very clear, and there is a temptation to think in psychological terms here. If that were what was intended, then Kung's answer would not amount to much, for what is psychologically effective varies from one person to the next, and is only accidentally, if at all, related to what is true.

There is, however, a further point to be made, which is even more central to my concerns. These passages from *Does God Exist?* illustrate my dilemma over 'incomprehensibility' very plainly. Where, and by what criteria, should such terms be introduced into our discussion? It is, to say the least, odd that someone who finds the matter of God's goodness so incomprehensible, or the presence of suffering so mysterious, should be prepared to speak with such firmness about God and his many qualities. One is rather put in mind of the character Eddie Fislinger in Sinclair Lewis's *Elmer Gantry*: 'Although Latin, Maths, Grammer and Poetry all raised problems for Eddie, there had never been a time since the age of twelve, when Eddie had not known how the Lord God would act, or why he had done this and not that.' Just as one wants to know how someone so ignorant about maths and grammar can be so knowledgeable about the ways of God, so, one wonders how an incomprehension of God's goodness can be combined with a clear assurance about God's omniscience, omnipotence and the degree of his care for details.

To push the point further, and to relate it to the main theme of this chapter, I must insist upon parity of treatment for God's moral qualities and for his metaphysical attributes. There is an element of doublespeak in discussing and defining God's attributes quite plainly while insisting upon the mystery of evil and the incomprehensibility of his goodness when confronted with evil and suffering. This inconsistency, I suggest arises because the problems of evil and suffering are introduced into the discussion later rather than earlier. They enter the arena only after the main lines of a theological, indeed theistic position, have been adopted. At that stage one is fully committed to a path which will result either in making remarks about God and his activities which contravene the bounds of the morally acceptable, or in risking the contamination of an intellectually disreputable *mysterium ex machina*. Neither path is acceptable and my alternative suggestion is that we should start with the phenomena of evil and suffering, and adopt my second criterion of moral acceptability as the benchmark of what may be said of God. However I must admit that to all intents and purposes this amounts to replacing 'the incomprehensibility of goodness' and 'the mystery of evil' with a fairly thoroughgoing theistic agnosticism. To that extent this will be a *via negativa* with a vengeance!

There is an important counterpoint to my argument, however, which must be considered. In a most interesting paper titled 'On the Form of "the problem of Evil"',[11] Roy Holland isolates and attacks the importation of a fourth premiss into the analysis of the problem of evil. Although this may appear to be very close to the strategy which I have adopted insofar as I too have doubted the wisdom of speculating about whether God has morally sufficient reasons for permitting this or allowing that, there are none the less fundamental differences between Holland and myself which must be uncovered. This should help to clarify the principles to which I am adhering and also to prepare the way for the next stage of the discussion.

Holland argues that to look for morally sufficient reasons in someone's activity or purposes 'presupposes membership of a moral community':

> But God is not a member of a moral community or of any community. To be sure there are small 'g' gods who have been conceived in that way, like those of the ancient Greeks:

such gods are like fairies. To credit the one true God with
having a moral reason for doing anything is to conceive Him
in the manner of Greek popular religion as a being among
beings instead of the absolute being who is the Creator of the
world. When 'God' is conceived as a one among many he
becomes subjectable to moral judgement. (p. 238)

The central issue at stake here concerns the connection
between looking for morally sufficient reasons for the presence of evil and suffering and introducing the ideas of mystery and incomprehensibility. In the earlier sections of this
chapter I have criticized those who have tried to ride both of
these horses by looking for morally sufficient reasons *as far as
they can*, and when they come to a terminus, invoking the
name of mystery and incomprehensibility. The connection
which Holland makes is that the reason for refusing to discuss the moral sufficiency of God's purposes in tolerating evil
is that it diminishes the element of mystery, understood as
'awesome wonder' (p. 241): such discussion expects of and
makes of God 'something commonplace' quite out of keep-
ing with taking seriously 'the idea of supreme goodness' and
our relation to it. Thus a fundamental principle for Holland is
that the goodness of God is such that it is to be approached
with the awe due to one who is *not* a member of a moral
community.

The implication behind Holland's argument is that what is
going on is the *subjection* of God to moral judgement in a way
that demeans God to a 'god', one amongst many. This of
course is one central theme in much argument around what
has come to be known as 'the Euthyphro dilemma': namely
is the will of God good because it accords with what is good,
or is what is good good because it accords with the will of
God? There is evidence that Holland would, if pressed, opt
for the latter and clearly there is a serious charge to be made
against my view – that I am 'subjecting' the will of God to
moral judgement. Whether my criterion 2 is a replay of one
side of 'the Euthyphro dilemma' is the subject matter of the
next chapter but before giving detailed consideration to that,
I wish to clarify my position *vis-à-vis* Holland and his attack

on those who look for 'morally sufficient reasons' for God's permission of evil.

Just as I have rejected the view that moves from our inability to find morally sufficient reasons which are adequate, to consequent affirmation of mystery and incomprehensibility, so also do I reject the view that the awesome mystery of God's supreme goodness is adequate grounds for refusing to apply to beliefs in and about God my second criterion – religious belief which runs counter to our moral beliefs is to that extent unacceptable. Within these limits I am of one mind with those who do raise questions about a God who permits evil. Where I disagree with Holland is that in one respect he makes the same move as Hick, Mitchell and Kung. He takes up the question of evil and suffering from an account of belief in God which in certain important respects is already delineated. The most important respect is that he 'is not a member of a moral community', by which Holland means that what we say of him need not conform to our accepted moral criteria. Now I can see what leads Holland to argue in this way, but even apart from my intention to begin with the question of evil and suffering rather than with an already formed account of the content of religious belief, I think that Holland has misrepresented the situation to himself and to others in two important respects.

In the first place he makes it plain that the real worry behind his warning that 'God is not a member of a moral community' is that not to think in this way is to think of God, 'by whom we are judged' as being 'submitted to our moral judgement'. I shall make my own position clearer by pointing out that the judgement arising from my second criterion is a judgement of beliefs about God rather than a judgement of God – in just the same way that Holland's judgement of the anthropomorphism of Greek religion, or of the 'tone' of Swinburne's remarks about evil, is itself a judgement of beliefs about God.

In the second place, and following from this, we must ask whether there are any grounds for arguing that it is not legitimate to reject specific accounts of God on moral criteria which have their relevance because of our confronting the facts of evil. Holland's article suggests two such grounds. The first which can be set aside pro tem fairly quickly, is that it is easy for such an outlook to be founded upon what he perceptively calls 'the ethics of indignation'. (How dare God . . .?) Now there is something odd in such a view and I have discussed aspects of this elsewhere, but at the moment it suffices to point out that to raise moral objections to specific claims about God is to be quite in accord with the refining of belief clearly going on in the Old Testament. The Book of Job, for example, amongst other things rejects certain accounts of the relation between God and evil and suffering. There are also many contemporary writers who would reject 'the ethics of indignation' and the implicit atheism of rebellion, but who would still stumble at affirming the moral acceptability of evil conceived as purposive. One does not have to move from the refusal to accept a morally destructive picture of God to asking 'How dare God . . .?'

In the end my disagreement with Holland is not substantially different from my disagreement with Hick, Mitchell and Kung, and it is over the question which is the theme of this chapter. Why should we invoke the terms 'mystery', 'incomprehensibility' and 'awe' in the discussion of evil and goodness in a way which deprives us of the right to ask further questions, and more specifically to apply criterion 2, while we do not seem equally constrained in the other firm judgements which we make about God? This is equally a problem for the ease with which Holland distinguishes between forms of belief such as his own and those of others which he rejects, as it is for the juxtaposition in Kung's talk of God's 'incomprehensible goodness' with a catalogue of the elements of God's paternal care for us.

A final footnote which prepares the way for the discussion of the relation between moral and religious beliefs is that nothing I have said denies the sense of the term 'mystery' encapsulated in the following two remarks from Holland's earlier paper 'Is Goodness a Mystery?' The first is from a conversation in which in this instance Wittgenstein is the speaker: the second is a later comment by Holland:

> Schlick says that theological ethics contains two conceptions of the essence of the Good. According to the more superficial interpretation. Good is good because God wills it; according to the deeper interpretation, God wills the Good because it is good.
>
> I think that the first conception is the deeper one; Good is what God orders. For this cuts off the path to any and every explanation 'why' it is good, while the second conception is precisely the superficial, the rationalistic one, which proceeds as if what is good could still be given some foundation. (p. 93)

> Why this goodness is what it is or why it should be present at all is left as the mystery it needs must be. When explanations are attempted of *this*, a movement of thought takes place of which I have offered illustrations. (p. 109)

Holland and Wittgenstein have been too ready to follow Schlick's exhaustive division, just as Schlick too readily reflects the structures of the Euthyphro dilemma. Of course, if it is an either/or, there are strong arguments in favour of this side. Suffice it to say that I do not accept here an either/or, and that as I shall show, this stance does not lead to attempts to diminish the 'mystery' of goodness by trying to give it foundations or explain why it is as it is.

3

Religious Belief and Moral Commitment

Is that which is holy loved by the gods because it is holy, or is it holy because it is loved by the gods?[1]

It might well seem that the high priority which I have given to my second criterion – 'a religious belief which runs counter to our moral beliefs is to that extent unacceptable' – amounts to no more and no less than answering Socrates' question to Euthyphro by insisting that what is holy is loved by the Gods because it is holy. Such a view is taken to be an insistence that moral beliefs are to be given priority over religious beliefs if there is a clash between the two, for it is assumed that one or other must be 'prior' or 'more fundamental'. The history of the discussion of religious and moral beliefs has been dominated by such an either/or, and it could seem as if I am accepting this construction of the issues at stake. In fact the view which I am trying to clarify and develop is in essential respects quite different, and it is important to be clear about this at the outset.

The first and indeed last point to be made – for it embraces all the others – is that I propose to follow the method laid down in the first two chapters: the method of natural religion or revisionary theology as I have redefined them. It is useful to recall two negative features of my approach. There is to be no appeal to revealed religious truths, and the structures of a foundationalist epistemology are to be set aside. The demands of the either/or of the *Euthyphro* discussion for the relationship between religious and moral beliefs is to that

extent weakened, for such theological and philosophical presuppositions lend weight to the suggestion that *either* moral
or religious beliefs must be prior the one to the other, by
suggesting ways of deciding in the case of possible conflict.
Thus someone who accepts that God has revealed his will
clearly to us, in the end will be bound to give priority to that
revelation should it conflict with our moral intuitions.
Equally, someone who accepts that all of our beliefs,
including the moral and the religious, ought to find their
appropriate level within an epistemological hierarchy which
rests upon sure and clear foundations, will be more sym-
pathetic to the *Euthyphro* demand for an either/or in this
context. At this stage the theological point about a revision is
more significant, but the philosophical point about 'foundations' will be further discussed in due course.

However, two further reminders are necessary. I have
already suggested that to some extent those who would
adopt the mantle of revisionary theology are thereby clothing
themselves with the intellectual constraints of their age. It
does seem to me that our age is one in which there is a degree
of both moral and religious confusion, and that in those
circumstances it would be folly to insist from the outset that
either the religious or the moral must be given logical priority. As I shall argue, there is an alternative and much less
dangerous way of proceeding. Finally, if as proposed under
criterion 3 'the acceptability of a form of religious belief is
related to its comprehensiveness in the sense which it makes
of our experience of the world in which we find ourselves,'
then a view of the relation between religious and moral
beliefs is to be *found* rather than assumed. To *begin* by accepting one or other of the options put to us in the question from
the *Euthyphro* is to settle the issue in advance of the very
exploration laid down as a pre-condition for the proper
formulation of our beliefs.

None the less, it might still be argued that my second
criterion does precisely that, and to combat such a charge I
must now offer an alternative construction of the relation
between the will of God and what is good.

Both in the question which is posed in the *Euthyphro* and in the following comment by Wittgenstein which I quoted in the previous chapter, a particular construction is given to the question of the relation between religion and ethics: 'Schlick says that theological ethics contains two conceptions of the essence of the Good. According to the more superficial interpretation, Good is good becuse God wills it; according to the deeper interpretation, God wills the Good because it is good.' Insofar as there is a clear question and issue here, it can be given a number of different forms. I shall focus upon two of these. On the one hand perhaps we are being asked whether appeal to religious premises (e.g. 'God wills it') can be allowed to settle whether some action is good: on the other hand perhaps we are being asked whether what we mean by 'the Good' is what is 'according to the will of God'. My suggestion is that if our concern is to give account of the relationship between religious and moral beliefs, answers to these questions will be of no help whatsoever – or, in the words of the Irishman in the story, 'If that's where you want to go, I wouldn't start here.'

It is important to distinguish between two different propositions:

(1) God always wills the Good;
(2) the God of Christian (or any other) theology always wills the Good.

The second proposition is synthetic. My second criterion – 'a religious belief which runs counter to our moral beliefs is to that extent unacceptable' – must be read and understood in the light of this. As such it is not involved in the questions raised by Socrates' cross-examination of Euthyphro, for it is a test of particular systems of religious belief, not of the goodness of God. It would be a test of the latter only if it were used as a criterion of the truth or falsehood of (1) 'God always wills the Good.' That use of the second criterion, however, could arise only if we believed that God wills something which runs counter to our moral beliefs. We could find ourselves in such a position only if we regarded ourselves as having a clear picture of what God wills (as distinct from what the Church, or the guru, or a particular book tells us that he wills) and found *that* in opposition to our moral beliefs or intuitions. My central question concerns how we could possibly come to have such a clear view of the will of God, apparently arrived at without reference to our moral sensibilities. My recommendation, or indeed prescription, is to avoid that state by concentrating our discussion on the second synthetic proposition about the God of Christian or any other theology.

This however leaves unanswered the legitimate question of the truth of the first proposition – (1) God always will the Good. The matter of the truth of this proposition is related to its status. My proposal is that it should be accorded the status of an analytic truth, and that as such the tests of the truth of (1) are those appropriate to analytic truths. The implication of this is that where (2) may be open to falsification in principle, which is at least in part empirically based, this is not so in the case of (1). Despite this, however, I do not wish to suggest that (1) is unimportant, or of 'merely' linguistic significance. The role of (1) is to assert a fundamental belief about the ultimate compatibility and indeed interdependence of moral and religious beliefs. It is a neat formula whose analytic status reflects the primary significance which it has in the system of ideas which this book is intended to define. It is also, however, a potentially very misleading formula, for it seems to be asserting a straightforwardly descriptive truth about the goodness of a being called God. This picture misleads us with regard to both the content and the staus of (1).

Little can be said of the content of (1) at this stage and consequently no final view can be taken of its truth. As will become increasingly apparent, the central aim of this study is to give content to claims such as those embodied in (1). If the conclusions validly reflect these intentions, then the analytic status of (1) will be confirmed as the meaning of it is delineated. For the time being the only content which can be given to (1) is, as already suggested, that it affirms a fundamental belief in the ultimate compatibility and interdependence of moral and religious beliefs. It will also, I shall argue, render inappropriate the claim that the one type of belief may be reduced to the other.

To summarize, the criterion of moral acceptability is a criterion applied to claims made by particular theologies, theologians or systems of religious belief. As such it does not involve enlistment on one side or the other of the *Euthyphro* argument, for the latter seems to involve claims about God, rather than about theologies. Largely, of course, this is the fault of theologians who have regularly failed to distinguish *theos* and theology. While there may be something of blasphemy in judging God, there is certainly nothing blasphemous in the judgement of theologies and theologians (or philosophers for that matter). Indeed I am prepared to defend the claim that (1) God always wills the Good, is analytically true, but the elaboration of this claim will be a painstaking and ardous journey. Whereas the impact of the so-called 'Euthyphro dilemma' has been to encourage the assumption that we know quite well and clearly what (1) means, in fact such clarity has to be achieved rather than assumed. We must work *towards* such clarity, for in its absence we cannot work *from* it.

The alternative position which I wish to defend and which is certainly compatible with the emphasis which I am placing on my second criterion, but which will require the further elucidation of that criterion, is that in periods of the discussion and development of religious belief, religious and moral beliefs are attached to one another in mutually modifying ways. The point is that my second criterion does not deny that moral beliefs might change under the impact of religious insights, and of course I am clearly endorsing the view that religious beliefs may well have to be modified by deepening moral awareness. Such a conversational view of the relation between religion and ethics is offensive only to those who believe that they have access to absolute or ultimate truth whether moral or religious. The dangers of such an outlook are precisely what Socrates is trying to bring home to the arrogant young Euthyphro. I am well aware of being open to misunderstanding, or even to the charge of relativizing, but my defence against such a charge must wait. Suffice it to say that my remarks so far do not commit me to the view that there are no moral or religious absolutes, but rather to the view that our awareness or knowledge of such absolutes will be at best limited and partial. Equally I am quite clear in my own mind that we may well have to decide and act in accord with beliefs which have the form of absoluteness while yet insisting upon the limitations of our knowledge and insight. For example, a man or a woman may follow a vocation which excludes much else in life while still allowing the possibility that they *might* be deluded.

However, I must give some more specific content to the idea of moral and religious beliefs in mutually modifying conversation. The first point is that we none of us enter into discussion of or reflection upon moral and religious questions with minds as unformed as the traditional Lockean *tabula rasa*. At whatever point in our lives we do reflect on these matters, we bring to our enquiry a ragbag of beliefs, emotions, half–beliefs, sentiments and uncertainties, on a variety of moral and religious questions. Wiping the slate clean to start afresh is not possible. We may well and should devise techniques for sorting and evaluating our intellectual and emotional clutter, but the way ahead is modification and reconstruction from within rather than complete demolition. What is true of the individual is equally true of historical movement and change. This is a matter of logic just as much as of sociology and psychology.

The stress which I am giving to this element of our conceptual and linguistic abilities has been discussed in a rather different context in Waismann's paper on 'Verifiability'.[2] Now I must immediately say that there is no evidence that Waismann would approve of my borrowing his expression 'open texture', but I propose to do so. Waismann applies it to empirical concepts and means 'that definitions of open terms are *always* corrigible or emendable'. I believe that there is an analogous characteristic of both moral and religious expressions and this is a central feature of all that I want to say about religious belief. There will be more detailed treatment of this in due course: suffice it to say for the moment that the question which Waismann asks of empirical concepts – 'Have we rules ready for all imaginable possibilities?' – has great force when applied to moral and religious ideas. If, as I should certainly argue, the ideas with which we operate in these contexts are also in principle revisable, then it is clearly possible for the moral and the religious to modify one another in a way that does not presuppose the absolute priority of the one or the other.

In the context of religion and morality this is a two-way process, and I shall substantiate my claims by giving examples of modification of religious views by moral views and vice versa.

Alastair MacIntyre gives an important but one-sided general argument here which bears close examination: 'my contention is that theism itself requires and presupposes both a moral vocabulary which can be understood independently of theistic beliefs and moral practices which can be justified independently of theistic beliefs'.[3] MacIntyre put the point far more strongly than I should, and I have considerable misgivings about his stress on the idea of the independent *justification* of moral beliefs. The issue to be emphasized, however, is the claim that theism requires a moral vocabulary which can be grasped and understood independently of theistic beliefs. MacIntyre constructs a very telling example to illustrate his thesis: if the only moral reason for doing something is that God commands it and if this is because goodness is defined as whatever God commands, then a theist would have lost the means of distinguishing between God and Satan.

> For God has been transformed by the proponents of this view into a Hobbesian sovereign whose title to legitimate authority rests not on his absolute paternal care, his goodness as a father, but solely on his power, and the devil's lack of such a title rests solely on his inferiority in respect of power . . . Christian theism in particular can scarcely tolerate this: to cite

only one example, the story of the temptation of Jesus by Satan with the offer of all the kingdoms of the world loses its point even as a parable unless God and Satan stand in a different moral relationship to power, in a sense of 'moral' which is our ordinary familiar sense.

The point is well taken, for if we are to understand the religious significance of the story, we must bring to it a grasp of at least some of the moral dimensions of the nature and exercise of power.

There are, however, aspects of MacIntyre's view which are less satisfactory. From the fact that we can and must bring a capacity to use moral concepts to our understanding of elements of religious belief, it does not follow that we may not come to believe that the moral and religious concepts are rather more closely connected than we had first imagined. There are many concepts which we can grasp and appeal to quite effectively while still having a comparatively limited picture of their logical geography. There is a limited but useful comparison here with the concept of a triangle, and of a straight line. We might well be able to operate accurately and effectively within certain contexts with both these ideas, without being aware that the sum of the angles of any triangle constructed on a base running from one end of a line to any point on it, is equal to the sum of angles on the same side of the line as the triangle, formed by the base of the triangle and the continuation of the line to its other extremity. In the moral case MacIntyre implies that we must have a *complete* grasp of and even justification for our moral vocabulary before the significance of certain crucial elements of theism can be grasped. This seems to me simply not to be true, for we can often well operate with concepts and terms without being in a position to give the sort of account of them which MacIntyre seems to demand. If this is true of terms such as 'triangle' and 'straight line' of which very precise formal definitions can be given, how much more so is it true of 'goodness' or 'justice'?

As MacIntyre has argued that certain religious insights and distinctions presuppose a grasp of a range of moral concepts, so also there are many examples of the modification of these religious ideas by pressure brought to bear on them by moral insights. The second chapter began with a reference to Plato's attack on the religious stories and beliefs of his contemporaries for their moral inadequacy. Ironically for Plato, a parallel theological critique was being carried on by the very poets whose freedom to express themselves he was contesting. Thus, for example, we find in Sophocles and Euripides a critique of the theology of their Greek contemporaries and forefathers which is carried on quite clearly in the light of moral insights. Equally clearly the prophetic books of the Old Testament deploy many moral points in religious and theological argument, and the book of Job includes a critique of the traditional accounts of the relation between an individual's suffering and his God. However, there are many instances also of the modification of moral belief in the light of religious insights.

That the relationship is one of *mutual* modification becomes even more apparent if we examine the interplay of theology and ethics in the teaching of Jesus. Consider the following passage: 'Ye have heard that it was said by them of old time Thou shalt not commit adultery: But I say unto you. That whosoever looketh on a woman to lust after her hath committed adultery already with her in his heart.' Commenting upon the above passage John Wisdom wrote that in these words,

> [Christ] put into our minds a modified concept of adultery and, by implication, a modified concept of robbery, of violence, of intolerance, of forgiveness. He thereby for better or for worse, increased our insight into ourselves and our demands upon ourselves. For before Christ spoke we could count ourselves far from adulterers and other sinners provided we had not done this or done that; but since he spoke we have felt we have no true picture of ourselves until we have looked within, searched our hearts.[4]

Now we must not allow the innocence of the sophistication of New Testament scholarship shown by this passage to obscure the important philosophical and theological insights which it contains. A moral belief is being modified here in a way that does not involve rejection of the original belief: a human being will not understand what it is to commit adultery (or violence, or robbery) in the heart, unless they already understand what it is to commit adultery (robbery, violence, etc.). The moral insight being offered presupposes and depends upon modifying an already existing moral belief.

Further, the modification in question is logically related to a modification that is basically theological. The relationship between man and God is being redefined. A legal picture which is oriented basically towards external and outward acts is being set on one side. In its place is substituted a picture of the relationship between God and man defined in terms of the inner life. The theology here modifies but does not discard the ethics. This latter point is extremely important today, as it was in the intellectural struggles of St Paul to do justice both to the innovations of the teaching and activity of Jesus and to his place in the development of the Jewish tradition from which he came. Equally, the subtleties of this view of religious and moral beliefs as 'mutually modifying' each other, avoid the foolish and dangerous excesses of those who might think that a religion of inwardness has nothing to with the moral unacceptability of adultery, violence, or robbery, which are external outward acts. The original moral beliefs in this case are not set aside: indeed there is a clear sense in which the new beliefs depend upon them.

Equally important is the realization that the change in belief and outlook invited is not at the expense of or counter to our moral sensitivities; rather the invitation is to change by extending our moral sensitivities. This pattern is, of course, quite the opposite of the Kierkegaardian interpretation of Abraham's response to what he believed to be a command from God.

The examples which I have outlined, in an attempt to give content to the idea of a 'mutually modifying' relationship between religious and moral beliefs, prompt a series of more general reflections on the nature of the concepts which are central to these beliefs.

I have already borrowed the term 'open texture' from Waismann, and although I must once again stress that in borrowing I am also changing the use of the term quite significantly, none the less there are some useful analogies between Waismann's account of the term as applied to empirical concepts, and my own as applied to moral and religious ideas.

> A term is defined when the sort of situation is described in which it is to be used. Suppose for a moment that we were able to describe situations completely without omitting anything (as in chess), then we could produce an exhaustive list of all the circumstances in which the term is to be used so that nothing is left to doubt; in other words, we could construct a *complete definition*, i.e. a thought model which anticipates and settles once for all every possible question of usage. As, in fact, we can never eliminate the possibility of some unforeseen factor emerging, we can never be quite sure that we have included in our definition everything that should be included, and thus the process of defining and refining an idea will go on without ever reaching a final stage. (p. 122)

If this is true of empirical concepts, *a fortiori* it is true of religious and moral concepts. Such a process of 'defining and refining' is precisely what is going on in the discussion of 'adultery in the heart'. Of course, much larger stakes are also at issue, but the point still holds for the moral idea. Part of the strength of the beliefs of major religious traditions rests on this capacity which some of their central terms have, to be modified and refined to meet circumstances and to live in contexts which would have been quite unimaginable when these ideas first took form.

This relates to a further point made in the first chapter where it was stressed that Christianity is a religion with a history and that because of the importance of some historical beliefs about its origins, it is a religion for which the idea of historical development is perculiarly significant. As the historical character of the Christian religion has been stressed, particularly in the nineteenth and twentieth centuries, so tensions have arisen between those who think the core of

Christianity is 'the faith once delivered', and those who lay emphasis upon the variety of forms which that faith has taken in different times and places. One element of the tension which arises from the historical character of the religion relates to the question of absoluteness and finality. The fear on the one side is that unless the finality of the content of faith is stressed, then there will be no transcendence in that belief: we shall be confined to the relative and changing insights of what is historical and immanent. Such a division of emphasis is an encouragement to the distractions of the 'Euthyphro dilemma' and the like, for that dilemma arises in part when we fail to do justice to the historical development of Christian belief.

My proposal is that the 'open texture' of moral and religious concepts is the basis for the possible reconciliation of both the historical and the absolute character of the concepts embodied in fundamental beliefs. That someone may believe in an absolute sense in the goodness of God is on such a view quite compatible with a realization that the account which one might give of that goodness is to some large extent conditioned by the stage in the development of the history of such a belief in which one finds oneself – both communally and individually. Thus to return to a point made earlier, I may insist that the proposition 'God is good' is analytically true, while accepting that the following proposition could at best be synthetically true: 'The God defined in my theology is good.' This is not a peculiarity of any theology which I may espouse, it is a feature of all theologies; just as a similar point can be made about all accounts of the nature of goodness. Thus one may not consider that the goodness of God is a matter for further discussion while still being moderately or even deeply uncertain as to whether one can give an adequate, let alone a *complete* account of the nature of that goodness. This, I believe, meets Holland's point about the absolute goodness of God while at the same time giving full play to my suggestion that the history of religious traditions can be understood better in terms of the mutual modification of the moral and the religious than in the confrontations of the 'Euthyphro dilemma'. Equally this point applies to the development of belief within an individual.

There are three points at which this conclusion relates to the general theme of this book. The first is that I hope that I have established the possibility of using the criterion, 'a religious belief which runs counter to our moral beliefs is to that extent unacceptable,' without committing myself to the view that moral beliefs are in some absolute sense prior to religious beliefs. Religious beliefs can be the basis for changing moral beliefs, but *only by pointing to alternative beliefs which are accepted as morally superior.*

The second point is that all that I have proposed here is compatible with, and is indeed a particular interpretation of, what is referred to by some theologians as human finitude. This is a point which will be amplified considerably in later chapters. The initial claim is that our finitude is recognized in our realization that our beliefs about God and about goodness are all subject to revision. However, being finite does not preclude the belief that our relative and shifting perceptions are insights into an order of things pointed to by the claim that God is good. At this point I can imagine a protest from Hick, Mitchell and Kung that this is the point of view lying behind their various discussions of 'mystery', 'incomprehensibility' and the problem of evil. However, I think not; but the reasons for this are still to be unfolded. My point is that our finitude applies equally to our various conceptions of God, as it does to our conceptions of goodness. Interestingly, a related point is made by H. L. Hart writing in a rather different and secular context:

> It is a feature of the human predicament (and of of the legislative one) that we labour under two connected handicaps whenever we seek to regulate, unambiguously and in advance, some sphere of conduct by means of general standards to be used without further official directions on particular occasions. The first handicap is our relative ignorance of fact; the second is our relative indeterminacy of aim. If the world in which we live were characterized only by a finite number of features, and these together with all the modes in which

they could combine were known to us, then provision could be made in advance for every possibility.[5]

Whereas in Hart's case this leads to implications for our view of legal formulae, as already suggested this will lead me *for moral reasons* to be far more agnostic in what I say about God than any of the three thinkers aforementioned.

One final comment is designed to meet a point which some might wish to raise. Apart from the fact that in outlining my position I have excluded the possibility of appeal to revelation, there are other reasons for finding such a proposed source of religious or moral absolutes unacceptable. Revelation at this level is always at best *our interpretation* of what we believe to be revealed. As such it is prey to all the difficulties of finitude and open texture. We may care to affirm that it is revealed to us that we must love our neighbour, or even that God is good, but the crucial question is how we are to or do understand this. My suggestion is that the understanding of such claims *never* makes progress at the expense of moral sensitivities. In fact, in an odd way the claim that God is good is a way of saying this.

4

God, Eternity and Agnosticism

I have already argued at some length in chapter 2 that if we choose as our starting point for theological reflection the experience of suffering and evil, the outcome must be a considerable degree of agnosticism about God. In this chapter I propose to argue two theses:

> (1) that there are other strong and specific grounds for severely restricting our traditional theistic ways of thinking;
> (2) that the case for a very strong form of agnosticism about God becomes irresistible if these difficulties are seen in the context set by a theology which starts from the consideration of evil and suffering;

These theses interact with one another, and they will be considered in tandem.

In chapter 2 I elaborated the proposal that there are constraints on what we may say of God set by our moral beliefs. If, as I proposed, we begin the discussion of what we may say of God by the consideration of the problems set by the presence of evil and suffering in the world, then these constraints are very severe indeed. It may well be argued that the adoption of such a starting point is in fact foolhardy and that the outcome will inevitably be a distortion of the truth. Perhaps it might be suggested, we need all of the resources of a developed account of belief in God in order even to dare to think about anything so difficult as evil and suffering. Would that such resources were legitimately available!

In this chapter my argument will be that even if we were to start from a traditional theological account of God, we would run into comparable difficulties. The problems which initially we found arising from our starting-point of evil and suffering all focussed upon the question of the personal attributes of God. The difficulty which we faced was that of finding ourselves unable to talk in clear and intelligible ways about the *purposes, intentions* or *motives* of an omnipotent, omniscient and good God. In the end a degree of mystery or incomprehensibility had to be built into our account of such a God. In itself this implied an element of agnosticism, but agnosticism of a rather *ad hoc* or random nature. There seemed a considerable discrepancy, for example, between what Kung thought it possible to affirm of the metaphysical attributes of God, and the care he took to qualify God's primary moral attribute – goodness – as 'incomprehensible'. The discrepancy, however, is not simply the result of a different starting-point – evil and suffering – for I believe that this latter simply highlights a rather more profound problem which traditional theism must face. The problem is in fact as old as theism and it is that of the relation of God to the world.

Whatever account is given of this relation, tensions emerge. These tensions support rather than eliminate the case for a strong element of agnosticism in what we say about God. In fact the very idea of saying things 'about God' does seem to me to lie at the root of the matter, but in order to substantiate this claim I must first elaborate a very central instance of these tensions. The point is this: if we are prepared to make assertions 'about God', then equally we must be prepared to answer questions 'about God'. Particularly, of course, we may ask whether God has a particular property or mode of being. In asking such questions we shall find adequate endorsement of the agnostic conclusions of the second chapter. If God is to be God, as distinct from a god, then God must in some sense be transcedent and eternal, yet it is precisely this claim which raises the most profound problems for Christian theism. Therefore, I propose to examine two different accounts of what it means to talk of God as eternal. Probably the most generally understood sense in which God is believed to be eternal is that of timelessness, as expounded for example by Boethius and Aquinas. An alternative view on the matter is to be found in Nelson Pike's *God and Timelessness*[1] and in Richard Swinburne's *The Coherence of Theism*.[2] Swinburne argues explicitly, and Pike implicitly, that talk of the eternity of God is better understood as talk of the everlastingness (or, as others prefer it, the sempiternity) of God. My argument is that difficulties arise in the published presentations of both of these accounts of the eternity of God.

Eternity and Timelessness

The classical definition of the eternity of God is found in Boethius: 'Eternity is the complete possession of eternal life all at once. (*tota simul*)' As part of my consideration of this account of God as eternal, I shall assume that to call someone or something timeless is to talk of what lacks both temporal location and temporal duration. The attractions of this view undoubtedly relate to the idea of God as immutable, and thus not dependent upon anything else for the manner of his existence. Theologians, however, generally have wished to add both omniscience and omnipotence to the attributes of such a timeless God. My own view is that, despite the ingenuity expended in showing the compatibility of these claims, the attempt will always fail, and I shall outline briefly my reasons for it.

It has been argued that if God is timeless, then he cannot be omniscient, for there are many important truths which a timeless being cannot know. Most crucially (as A.N. Prior has argued) a timeless being's knowledge would be restricted 'to those truths, if any, which are themselves tenseless'.[3] That is to say, such a God could not know what is happening *now*, nor what will happen tomorrow, nor what happened yesterday. If such a claim is true, then it would seem to eliminate the idea of God's *fore*knowledge, and this will have the advantage that it avoids at least some of the difficulties of the compatibility of belief in God with the belief that in some sense at least the future actions of human beings are free. The cost of this is the claim that God is omniscient. In an interesting contribution to this debate, Paul Helm has argued that it is not incoherent to claim that a timeless knower could be said to foreknow a particular action or event. 'What I wish to claim is that in these circumstances the concept of foreknowledge applies not to a timeless knower's knowledge of certain events or actions, but to a temporal agent's *recognition* of timeless knowledge.'[4] The implication of this is that whereas it would not be intelligible for a timeless knower to claim 'I foreknow that A', where A is an event or action, it is intelligible for a temporal being to say of a timeless knower 'He foreknows that A'. Helm suggests the following paraphrase: '(i) At a time before this time (the time of (i)'s utterance) the statement 'T timelessly knows A' (where T refers to the timeless knower, and A is an event future to the time of the statement's utterance) is true.' Within the terms of the discussion upon which he is engaged, i.e. whether a timeless knower's knowledge could be reasonably spoken of by a temporal being as foreknowledge, Helm's account seems to me to be legitimate. The cost in this case, however, is that all the difficulties in reconciling God's foreknowledge with human freedom reassert themselves. There have been a number of attempts to reconcile these, but to pursue them at the moment would be a diversion.

The two possibilities outlined above are: either we accept that there are considerable limitations to be set to the truths which a timeless knower may be said to know, but thereby allow at least the possibility of human freedom; or we accept an account such as Helm's and with it the possible consequence that a timeless knower could know now e_1, where e_1 is whether I shall leave the house before or after 8.15 tomorrow morning. That is to say, the concept of an omniscient timeless God is not without its problems. However, these problems, are, as I shall show in due course, rather deeper than has been acknowledged so far in this discussion. They concern what it could mean for a timeless being to know *anything*, let alone to know everything. From this follows an even broader question of what relationship an eternal (timeless) God could have to history.

This issue may helpfully be approached by considering whether a timeless God might be omnipotent. Would any limitations be set to the kinds of things which God might be capable of doing, specifically because he is regarded as being timeless? The limitations seem to me to be very considerable indeed.

If God is timeless, then it is difficult to see how he could effect changes in the temporal order. This seems to apply equally to events within creation, as well as to the event (if it is one) of Creation. In order to effect, even by initiating it, what happens in a time-sequence (history), it would seem that one must be or become, if not part of it in the sense of temporally extended, at least *locatable* within it. I am not here making the point that the individuation of events is only possible if they are conceived as belonging to a single time-series: discussion of this issue will follow in due course. The point here is that if an event which is part of the time-series to which we belong, i.e. is part of our history, then, if that event is to be explained as an act, then whether the agent be Endersby the post-office clerk, or God, prima facie that agent must be locatable within that time series. It is a legitimate step to point out that being *capable* of acting in history presupposes being locatable within the time-series of history. The definition of timelessness with which we are working excludes temporal location; and is therefore one which excludes the possibility of being in the type of connection with events necessary for being regarded as bringing them to be. The same point applies to the theological idea that God preserves the various states of affairs which constitute creation.

One possible modification of the conclusion that a timeless God cannot bring about changes within history is to be found in the suggestion that the idea of God might move believers to act in specific ways and that therefore there is an extended sense in which a timeless God can affect the course of history. This would, of course, still limit God's activity considerably and would certainly rule out traditional notions of omnipotence. It could also be protested that it is not God who brings about change, but only the idea or possibly contemplation or awareness of God which affects the course of history. This would be unduly fastidious, however, for it does seem quite conceivable that one might truthfully say that the beauty of the valley was a major factor in the defeat of the planning application or that the demands of justice settled the issue, without acknowledging the necessity of rephrasing these in some such terms as 'the chairman's sense of . . .'. Even so, the idea of the timelessness of God does seem incompatible with traditional notions of omnipotence, and in so doing does set further constraints to possible answers to the broader question of the relation of a timeless God to history.

As can be inferred from these brief discussions of omniscience and omnipotence, some of the major problems arising from belief in an eternal, in the sense of timeless, God arise when we attempt to attribute to such a God the characteristics or activities of a person. In talking of 'persons' I am not wanting to enter the maze of Trinitarian theology. Rather the issue is whether or not timeless existence is a conceivable form of existence for a person, or even a being. The problem can be exemplified by quoting a passing comment from Paul Helm's paper. In dismissing the possibility of a trivial objection to his way of phrasing a point, Helm adds: 'Nothing, of course, hangs on the *utterance* of "I foreknow A" and it may be thought artificial to suppose that a timeless knower could utter anything. If so we can substitute "truly represent to himself that", for "utter" or "state"' (p. 525). The implied difficulty is, of course, that 'uttering' is most obviously understood as the action of a corporeal being, requiring vocal chords, lips, tongue and so on. Helm avoids the obvious ways out of the difficulty of what can be meant here, and rather than simply stating that the notion is to be understood analogically or symbolically, he eliminates the first order spatial references by rephrasing 'utter' as 'truly represents to himself'.

Certainly this removes the discomfort of the spatial connotations of 'utter', but it fails to recognize the more radical implications of talking of a timeless being. The point here is that we are not constrained simply to limit ourselves to the notion of a non-corporeal action, but rather we are in pursuit of the wild goose of a non-tensed action, one that does not involve the possibility of temporal co-ordinates being given to it. Such is inconceivable.

Actions essentially belong to time. They involve change, and as such are receptive of being located in a time-series (indeed, I should argue, if they are real rather than fictitious, in the time-series of which our lives are part). Here we arrive at the heart of the limitations which the concept of timelessness, as it is understood by the writers to whom we have already referred, imposes upon the idea of God. It excludes the possibility of action, not just *corporeal* action, but *any* action.

Thus such a God is not simply not active in history: he is not active at all. The implications for theism and religious belief are far-reaching. A timeless being cannot utter, but neither can he represent to himself. He cannot physically make or create, but neither can he deliberate, reflect, anticipate or intend, for these are all essentially temporal notions implying both duration and temporal location. He cannot, of course, remember or predict, suspect or confirm; nor is it easy to grasp what timeless love really can be. The question which inevitably arises concerns what sense, if any, could be attached to the claim that a God who cannot do any of these could be regarded as a person, or even as personal. The corollary relates to whether or not such a God would meet the needs of religion.

The conclusion which I draw from this discussion of the account of the eternity of God as the timelessness of God is that whatever the religious attractions of the idea, it cannot be combined with belief in an omnipotent, omniscient, active God.

Eternity and Everlastingness

For reasons of the sort discovered in the previous section of this chapter, a number of philosophers and theologians have either severely modified or actually rejected the doctrine of the timelessness of God. One of the most recent and interesting attempts to give an account of belief in God as a temporal being is to be found in Swinburne's book *The Coherence of Theism*. There it is argued, both explicitly and implicitly, that properly understood a coherent account of belief in God preserving at least something of the belief in God's omniscience, his omnipotence, and the type of activity compatible with talking of God as a personal ground of being – can be given if God is understood as a temporal being. If this is so, then considerable intellectual advantage will be found in preferring the view that God is temporal to the belief in his timelessness. I propose to argue that the gain is more apparent than real, and I shall do so by considering the content, according to this view, which can be given to the ideas of God knowing and of God acting.

In the matter of God's omniscience, certain points are not disputed by Swinburne. For example, he would not disagree with Helm's conclusion that if God is correctly believed to have foreknowledge of human actions, then that would limit, or remove completely, any possibility of human freedom. Swinburne's solution is to propose a modified account of omniscience which excludes future free actions from the range of what may be known:

> A person P is omniscient at a time t if and only if he knows of every true proposition about t or an earlier time that it is true *and* also he knows of every true proposition about a time later than t, such that what it reports is physically necessitated by some cause at t or earlier that it is true. (p. 175)

Initially it is important to note that the omniscience of such a
God is considerably less than Swinburne explicitly acknow-
ledges. It may seem that to grant even modified omniscience
(the knowledge of all events which are 'physically necessit-
ated by some cause') is to grant a great deal. If one is a
determinist, that, of course, allows knowledge of all events;
but if, as Swinburne hints, a belief in free human action
which is not either trivial or compatible with *determinism* is
legitimate, then a *consequence* of this is that what God knows
about the future will progressively diminish as human technology increases. For example, on this proviso, ever since
human beings have been in a position to land any form of
projectile on the surface of the moon, God cannot, on Swinburne's definition, have had any future knowledge of the
state of the surface of the moon. Indeed since it is conceivable
that human beings might have developed the technology to
do this much earlier than they did, then God could not have
been in a position to make many knowledge-claims about the
future at all. Claims about Haley's comet might still be safe
from the contamination or interference of human technology, but it could be simply a matter of time till someone
harnesses its advertising capacity by introducing colours or
form into its 'tail'. It is not necessary to spell out in any
further detail just how widespread the influence of one free
human act can be in limiting the knowledge of such a God,
for the restrictions which this view places on God's omniscience extend far beyond the generally trivial example of his
knowledge of the surface of the moon.

Even more basic, however, is the difficulty of giving a
clear account of what the knowledge of an omniscient temporal being could be like, even if one were to argue that
included in such knowledge is knowledge of human actions.
The difficulty may be put in this way: when we talk of the
knowledge which we temporal human beings have, there is a
whole series of connections and distinctions which we make
and which are built into the texture of our life and language.
In the view being examined – that belief in an omniscient
temporal being is coherent – many of these connections have
been cut. Some of these have been severed by postulating a

non-spatial being, and some by postulating an omniscient being who is none the less temporal. In order to deal adequately with the former, I should have to divert the discussion away from temporality to a consideration of Swinburne's arguments concerning the possibility of giving an account of personal identity over time which does not presuppose bodily continuity. Since I have some sympathy with the points being made by Swinburne in this section of his book, and since also it would involve a substantial digress from my concern with temporality, I shall restrict myself as far as possible to issues arising from the speculation that God is a temporal being.

As is clear from much contemporary philosophical writing on this subject, including Swinburne's book, worries about the coherence of belief in the omniscience of God have focused primarily on the idea of foreknowledge, and to a lesser extent on knowledge expressed in propositions of the form 'I am now turning into the South Circular'. There has been a comparative dearth of discussion of what it would be for a temporal omniscient knower to have knowledge of the past. Attention to this issue can help throw into relief some of the difficulties inherent in the discussion of omniscience.

For all temporal knowers there has to be a distinction, not simply between past, present and future, but also between knowledge of what is past, what is present and what is future, and in this part of the discussion I wish to restrict myself to cases of knowledge that, for example (1) there was a rainstorm in Edinburgh on 16 September 1978; (2) there is not a rainstorm in Edinburgh now; and (3) there will not be a rainstorm in Edinburgh tomorrow. Assume that each of these true claims is made on 19 September 1978, and that in each case adequate evidence of the truth of these claims is available to the person making the claims. For human beings, the grounds for (1) and (2) could be of two different sorts; on the one hand they might be present in Edinburgh on the day in question and be aware of the heavy rain falling; or on the other they might base their knowledge on reliable reports. In the case of God, such knowledge is not generally presumed

to be based upon a celestial intelligence agency, therefore it
would seem that if, as Swinburne intends, we are to make
any sense of the claim that he knows these truths, we shall
have to do so in terms of a picture of God somehow being
aware, i.e. in terms of knowledge by acquaintance rather
than by description. Although this is already beginning to
call to mind the type of trap set by Philo for Cleanthes[5] when
he encouraged his postulations with his 'Add, a mind *like the
human*', let us persevere to see where the picture of an omniscient temporal knower leads.

Leaving aside the fact that God is not a spatial being, we
may find considerable difficulties even in his proposed
temporality. As a temporal being God must clearly be in a
position to distinguish between remembering what has happened, and being aware of what is happening. Yet, granted
also that it is proposed that he is omniscient, what account
could be given of this? In the case of human beings there are
two general ways in which we might point to the distinction
between remembering an event and being aware of an event.
One such way is degree of certainty: aware of our own
fallibility in both contexts, it just is the case, and reasonably
so, that we are prepared to attach a greater degree of certainty
to our knowledge-claims about what we are attending to
now, than to our knowledge-claims about what we were
attending to yesterday. Other factors being equal, the past-
ness of X is an additional potential source of our being in error
about X. Clearly in the case of an omniscient temporal
knower, such an element would not be present as one of the
marks of distinction between remembering and being aware.

A second way in which we might try to give some account
of the difference between claims based on remembering and
claims based on being aware, would be in terms of the checks
which we might carry out in providing justification for such
claims. In the case of what we claim about what we are now
aware of, the checks might consist of looking more closely,
pinching ourselves to see if we are awake, asking anyone else
who happens to be there what they thought, etc. In the end,
however, claiming to know would involve being directly

aware in a particular way modified perhaps by these checks. In this case the postulated omniscient being would not have to undertake equivalent bodily or perspectival checks; but in essence his knowledge too would involve being directly aware. (Indeed it is difficult to avoid the conclusion that it would simply be being directly aware.) In the case of remembering what has happened, however, there is a marked divergence. For human beings there is a series of checks available in principle, and in the absence of these we should not be inclined to talk of knowledge (nor, if we regard it as an achievement verb, of 'remembering'). These checks all involve appeal to what we are aware of now, including the reports of others, records at the weather office, the state of one's roses, etc.; and one important feature here is that we may not, and indeed in some cases *could* not, have been aware of this evidence when, for example, the rain was falling in Edinburgh.

In the case of a postulated omniscient God, as we have seen, such appeal to indirect evidence is excluded. There are no equivalent checks. In his case, his remembering that it rained in Edinburgh on 16 September last is not differentiated from his awareness of the rainstorm on 16 September last by requiring supplementation from other sources in order to become the basis for a knowledge-claim. In other words, in certain contexts, and concerning certain sorts of knowledge, human beings draw a clear distinction between remembering and being aware, in the way in which appeal to other sources or not as the case may be is regarded as important. In the case of our omniscient temporal knower, however, no such appeal is relevant. In his case, if the notion of a check on knowledge of past events is to have any significance at all, it could only be in terms of the awareness one had being without fault. That could only be done by 'regenerating' the awareness, and checking the details of one's awareness.

The problem then is this: how could God distinguish between remembering an event X, and being aware of an event X? If, to put it colloquially, God has 'twenty-twenty' recall, what account can we give of the difference between

God remembering and God being aware. If, as is being postulated, God's knowledge is immediate in the sense of not even being mediated through sense organs, and if also it is direct in the sense of by acquaintence rather than by description, is there anything in the manner or content of being aware which for such a knower, could differentiate between rehearsing or recalling the past and being aware of the continuing present? It will not do simply to claim that somehow the difference is in the content of what one is aware of, the present being the present and therefore actual, the past being the past and therefore in a parallel sense no longer actual. As in a different context Berkeley was well aware, in order to distinguish between what can only be called two sets of 'awareness', it is not sufficient simply to classify one set as actual and one as non-actual: one has to give the criteria according to which such distinctions are made. Berkeley's difficulties, although derived from accounting for *human* mental activity, are instructive, as is his failure to overcome them. On the one hand one attempt which he made was to offer criteria such as strength, distinctness, orderliness and coherence. Now criteria such as these are ruled out by the nature of the case; for, on the one hand, the remembered events are known to have taken place and are therefore neither more nor less orderly and coherent than events known to be taking place. On the other hand the lack of strength and distinctness in our memories could only be a sign of the weakness and fallibility of finite beings. Alternatively, his further attempt to account for the distinction involved positing a God of the type whose very coherence is at the moment under discussion. He did realize, however, that it is not satisfactory to distinguish awareness of the actual from awareness of the non-actual simply in terms of the distinction between what is present and what is absent; for that itself is a problematic distinction.

The conclusion of this argument rests on the fact that an omniscient temporal being must have knowledge of both past and present events. Unless such an omniscient temporal being is content simply to equate what has happened with what seems to him to have happened – and that would be unacceptable for a variety of reasons – then, in principle, some checks must be possible. If his knowledge is immediate and direct, then checking procedures can only involve scrutinizing what I have referred to as his 'awareness of the past event' and his 'awareness of the present event'. If both 'awarenesses' amount to knowledge, as I have suggested that they do, then the usual criteria which can be used to distinguish awareness of the past from awareness of the present will not apply. What sense then can be made of such a distinction? Significantly, for all their other weaknesses, accounts of the knowledge which a timeless knower has of past, present and future, embodied in talk of *tota simul*, at least recognise this difficulty.

There are of course many other ways in which accounts of belief in God, understood as belief in an omniscient temporal knower, can be challenged. My intention here has been to show that, even granted a series of presuppositions about how to approach these questions, unresolved difficulties remain. With appropriate modifications, similar problems could be uncovered about distinguishing between an omniscient temporal knower's awareness of the present, and his knowing relationship to the future.

It might none the less be argued that the belief that God is a temporal rather than timeless being has the considerable advantage that at least a temporal being can be conceived of as acting. My argument will be that this supposition holds only if we ignore the subtle damage done to the concept of an action by assuming that the temporal being in question is also omnipotent. Swinburne spells out the implications of such an assumption, and in so doing specifies three different types of action which may be attributed to such a God: 'The theist claims that God brings about some things himself and makes (i.e. brings it about that) other beings bring about other things, and permits other beings to bring about yet other things' (p. 139). I shall comment on each briefly and then raise a general question about the sense of the term 'action' being used here.

As an example of the first type of action (which otherwise we might *prima facie* imagine to be typical of human action), Swinburne suggests 'creating a universe *e nihilo*'. This is indeed an exceedingly high standard to set for 'bringing about some things himself', and Swinburne agrees that human beings do not have the power to do this. In a very puzzling use of the word 'picture', he suggests that

> It is, however, fairly easy to picture what it would be like for them to have such a power. If I could just by so choosing produce a sixth finger or a new fountain-pen (not made out of pre-existing matter) I would have the power to bring matter into existence. (ibid.)

It is difficult to see what the point, or indeed sense, of this example is. It cannot surely be intended as a help to 'picturing' what God's activity is like, for if it is difficult to picture him creating *e nihilo*, it is not obvious that it will be easier to picture the managing director of Parker Pens, or a shop steward at British Leyland, doing so. The point here is that the invitation of 'picture' in this context is by no means easily interpreted, and could simply amount to the invitation to image a series of temporally connected, but otherwise apparently disjointed, scenes.

The second type of action attributed to God is, however, more central to the present discussion. According to Swinburne's account this seems to be at the heart of God's present relationship to his creation. God brings about 'the operation of natural laws'. This is a version of the traditional claim that God continues to hold the universe in existence 'by making its past states bring about subsequent states'. This is a very far-reaching conception, and when Swinburne argues 'that things have the effects in accord with natural laws which they do is, for the theist, itself an act of God' (p. 140), he comes very near to saying that everything that happens either is an act of God, or that it requires an act of God as a condition of its happening. (The one possible exception would be that for a mind-body dualist it is perhaps conceivable that there might be a sub-class of human acts – thinking, imaging, etc.

– which did not in any straightforward sense require the operation of natural laws.) The point of the distinction here is that whereas Swinburne seems to limit the activity of God to bringing about the effects of, for example turning the ignition-key, the very act of turning the ignition-key itself requires the operation of natural laws which connect the movements of nerve-endings, bone, muscle and so on.

This becomes particularly important as we note further types of action attributed to God: '[God] "permits" or "allows" an agent Q to bring about S if he brings it about that nothing stops Q from bringing about S.' (ibid.) The distinction between what God actively brings to be and what he permits has been a very important one in the history of theology, not least in so far as it has been related to the distinction between what God intends and approves on the one hand, and what he simply permits on the other. It is of significance in the discussion of the problems of evil and suffering. What Swinburne's account achieves, however, is an erosion of the distinction. If God permits one man to kill another (Swinburne's example), this is not a lack of activity on God's part; for according to Swinburne God must bring it about not simply that the natural laws necessary for connecting intention to the physical movement which causes the death, as well as for connecting pressure of fingers and asphyxiation, are not impeded, but in fact that each step in the process continues according to plan. In any court of law, morally imperfect though it be, a much lesser degree of co-operation would constitute grounds for conviction as an accomplice; and many a war criminal has been found guilty of being implicated in the death of others at a much greater distance than that. The *sangfroid* implicit in such a conception of God is morally grotesque.

The general point which I wish to make about acts of God is that they are incredibly difficult to individuate. Certainly there are problems about the individuation of human actions; but on the whole it would not be regarded as controversial to claim that of the events which do take or which have taken place, there are some which are clearly not my actions or the

consequence of my actions. The nature of the limitation
implicit in this should not however be obscured by the truth
that my power and capabilities are limited. Certainly that sets
limits to what *I* can do, but the point at issue is not óne of
individual capacities: it is rather one of what it is that is
legitimately characterized as 'an act of . . .'. My argument is
that amongst other conditions which apply, one very basic
one is that we may individuate this act of President Carter
both from the acts of other agents and also from Carter's
other acts. Now the ties which bind this area of history to
President Carter in such a way as to legitimate the description
'President Carter invited the President of Egypt to Camp
David', are very complex indeed; but the assumption implicit
in attempting to clarify what these ties are, is that there
should be a unique relationship between Carter and this area
of his and our history. Thus, for example, the relationship
which Carter has to that area of his history which we describe
as 'inviting the President of Egypt to Camp David' is quite
distinct from the relationship which he has to that area of his
history which we describe as 'inviting the Prime Minister of
Israel to Camp David'. Amongst other things, standard cases
of the ascription of actions to President Carter, or to anyone
else, assume at a very basic level notions such as 'being aware
of', 'paying attention to', and so on. Without being able to
tie even very general descriptions such as this to areas of
President Carter's experience, it is difficult to see what could
be meant by attributing actions to him. It is true that there are
non-standard cases of attributing actions to someone such
that we say, 'He wandered through the city without paying
attention to where he was going,' or – a different type of case
– 'She was unaware of the effect she was creating.' I should
want to stress, however, that these are non-standard or
derivative cases whose treatment will to some extent depend
upon the account given of standard examples of the attribution of actions.

   Consider now the case of proposed acts of an omnipotent
temporal being responsible for the range of acts specified by

Swinburne. At this moment I can hear clocks ticking, birds whistling, a car engine being turned over, heavy traffic in the distance, leaves (several hundred) rustling in the breeze; I am engaged in the series of movements involved in writing; someone outside is sweeping the pavement; and doubtless several thousand million other human beings are engaged upon this or that activity. Now as we have seen, in each individual case myriad 'acts of God' are required. There is no sense in which such an omnipotent temporal being can be described as having a unique relationship to the area of history – his and ours – concerned. There comes a point where the sheer volume of 'God's activity' so detaches the idea of 'an act' even from basic notions such as 'awareness' and 'attention', that the attempt to understand how the other more complex elements of the concept of action apply to 'an act of God' becomes a task which has no shape.

A rather different way of approaching these problems would simply be to ask, in terms of one current theological fashion, what 'model' we are to adopt in discussing the activity of such a God. The frenzy implicit in the anthropomorphic picture which emerges is sufficient itself to bring about a case of theological dizziness. Perhaps it is through some such experience as this that religious thinkers of different periods have been led respectively to explore deism and process philosophy.

In summary, I have examined the proposal that God's eternity, thought of as sempiternity, is more tolerant of the ideas of knowing and acting which seem to be required by a belief in the omniscience and omnipotence of God. My conclusion, however, is that the tolerance is at best prima facie, and that thus used, the concepts of knowing and acting become detached from the series of distinctions and connections which give them the sense that they have. Thus the eternity of God understood as the sempiternity of an omniscient, omipotent being is neither philosophically clearer nor religiously more adequate than the proposed alternative of a timeless knowing agent.

Conclusions

It might well be argued that the difficulties to which I point are already well known in the Christian tradition. Indeed Maurice Wiles comments on this while admitting: 'There may be grave difficulties in making sense of some of the more directly personal ways in which Christians speak of God. Indeed almost the whole of Christian theology could be presented as a continuing struggle with just that issue.'[6] He does insist however that 'we have no cause to fear that the personal language itself is altogether out of place.' The crucial question, as he agrees, is how one can validate any such claims made of God.

If we use personal terms to describe God, then we have already made one assumption which in the present enquiry is still open to question – namely, that in some sense the word 'God' either names or provides an individuating description. I do not think it is necessary here to take a view on the long-standing disagreement between those for whom the word names, and for whom it describes. It is sufficient for the moment to point to the common assumption held by both camps that the word individuates. It is because theists have thought in this way that the problems of the relation between God and the world have taken the particular form that they have. This way of thinking, I have argued, leads via the consideration of God's eternity to a series of (insoluble?) problems about the claims that God acts, or indeed that any personal qualities or attributes are his at all. Now once these problems are recognized, there are various ways in which we can try to circumvent them – via a doctrine of analogy, or a theory of metaphor, etc. – but for now I wish to recall the context of our present discussion.

In the second chapter I questioned the practice of some theologians and philosophers who in the face of evil and suffering talk of the 'mystery' and 'incomprehensibility' of God's moral attributes while apparently having less difficulty with the traditional metaphysical attributes of God. In fact the problems recognized by the use of terms such as 'mystery' are constituted in part by the acceptance of the traditional picture of an all-knowing, all-powerful active God. The case for constituting the problems in this way, and for so relegating God's moral attributes, is only as strong as the clarity of our account of God's metaphysical attributes. I hope that I have demonstrated that our account of these is far from clear.

The conclusion to be drawn from this is not – at least not yet – that we can be clear about God's moral attributes but not about his metaphysical ones. Quite to the contrary, I am suggesting that the case for agnosticism and for appeal to the *via negativa* is both cumulative and compound in character.[7]

Part II

The Eternal in Human Life

5

Theology: the Articulation of the Possible

Metaphysicians of a theological turn of mind, and theologians of a metaphysical disposition, have at least this much in common: the systems of ideas which they have constructed and commended have been in essence an account of the relations between three basic elements or building-blocks – God, the world, and self. The character of the resultant metaphysical or theological system has been an expression of the varying emphases on one or other of these, and of the *ordo cognoscendi* implied between them. The possible range of combinations, permutations and qualifications is at least as extended as the history of thought; but if a moment's over-simplification is tolerable, then there are three different emphases of approach to the question of how to formulate a way of thinking adequate to the task of living.

In the first place the theologian may emphasize the view of theology as talk or thought about God. Most traditional forms of theism belong here. The stress is upon the picture of God whose existence is objective in the sense of independent of both the world and the thoughts of human beings. This is true of Aquinas, who insists of theology: 'That God is the subject of this science should be maintained.'[1] And so too of Calvin, who begins the *Institutes* with an extended discussion 'Of the Knowledge of God the Creator', and also of Barth for whom the beginning and end of dogmatics is the self-revealing God: '[Scripture] absolutely insists upon being regarded from the side of its subject, God. It is the revelation of Him who is called *Yahweh* in the O.T. and *theos* or concretely *kurios* in the N.T.'[2] Inevitably in any such approach which is philosophically alert, the discussion soon comes to the realization of just how difficult such a task is, but even there the distinguishing feature of this emphasis lies in the ultimate focus and intention of saying what can be said about God as clearly as possible.

The second general emphasis is upon the world, by which I mean the world which we human beings experience. As in other emphases there are many variations possible here. I shall mention two extremes, one of which leans towards an emphasis upon God, the other leaning towards the emphasis upon man or self. In the former category one can quite certainly place the particular form of pantheism to be found in Spinoza. In his renowned *Deus, sive natura* (God, or nature) Spinoza gives quintessential expression to the insistence that Metaphysics and theology cannot have as their aim knowledge or even talk of a God who exists independently of the world; for he argues that there is only one primary kind of stuff, or substance, and that the picture of a God wholly independent of the world would presuppose the duallism of two primary substances. Clearly such an emphasis will produce a theology very different from that of Aquinas or Calvin. Indeed in Spinoza's case it led his contemporaries to accuse him, wrongly I believe, of atheism.

The second example under this general category which I offer looks rather towards the emphasis upon self or mind. This is the approach to theology which gives primary attention to how the world can be seen or experienced. On this view the proper impetus to and legitimation of theology comes from the fact that the world can be 'seen as' created, or 'as' providentially ordered. In its reductionist form this view implies that that is all that there is to it, and that there is no God above and beyond this. However, unless a full-blooded pantheism is adopted, this view is usually moderated by a basic empiricism which implies that there may well be a God just beyond the horizon of our perceptions. In different ways Wisdom, Hick and the Philo of part XII of Hume's *Dialogues* have offered views of this type.

The emphasis on the third building-block of theology, self, can show itself in at least two radical forms which insist on the one hand, for example, on offering a projectionist theory of what the meaning of statements about God amount to; or on the other, upon a strongly existentialist theory which in extreme form might equate belief in God with a particular form of self-development or self realization. Indeed the two forms sketched can be combined, as they are I believe in Don Cupitt's two most recent books.[3] They are, however, more often associated in the one case with theories such as those of Feuerbach or Freud, and on the other with some of the more extreme of Bultmann's writings on the concept of faith. Characteristically, theologies which stress this emphasis tend always towards subjectivist and often towards relativist positions.

What I have offered in these three sketches fails classification as 'parody' only in so far as I stress that I am simply outlining in very general terms three different tendencies which we may find in varying degrees within theological and metaphysical systems. These three tendencies can be correlated with the three central building-blocks of the history of the overlap between theology and metaphysics – God, the world, and self. The complexities of theological and metaphysical disagreement could, I believe, be traced out in terms of the differing relations between these blocks found in each proposed system of ideas. Respectively, each of the emphases can be characterized as follows:

(1) theology is talk about God;
(2) theology is talk about the world, for example that is identical with God or that it can be 'seen as' a creation of God;
(3) theology is talk about us, for example that belief in God is a form of self-knowledge or self-realization, or that God is a projection of our wishes or our ideals into the external world

I wish to propose an alternative view – not one which discards these elements or building blocks completely, but one which begins by defining itself in terms quite distinct from these:

(4) theology is the articulation of the possible.

I must devote the remainder of this chapter to elaborating and defending this view.

In the first four chapters, and particularly in the second and fourth, I developed a cumulative case for reinstating into theological and religious discussion strong elements of agnosticism and of the *via negativa*. The difficulties which led me to this conclusion focussed upon the moral and metaphysical attributes of God and on the assumption that the word 'God' either names an individual or incorporates into its meaning an individuating description. These same problems point towards the value of exploring an account of theism which demands an absolute minimum of commitment to the idea of God as an individual, a being, and *ipso facto* a person. Shocking as such a view may appear to some, it has always been an element of the Judeo-Christian tradition whether in terms of the Schoolman's definition of God as 'Being *qua* Being' or Paul Tillich's insistence that, 'It is as atheistic to affirm the existence of God as it is to deny it.'[4] In each case is implicit a very deep reservation about the identification of God as an individual, let alone a person.

My argument will be that in the elaboration of the view of theology as 'the articulation of the possible', much of what is central to theistic belief will be retained, and the distressing problems of the sense which can be made of the moral attributes of God, outlined in the second chapter, and the metaphysical attributes discussed in the fourth, will be given a new and less intractable form. I believe also that a strong emphasis on agnosticism and on the *via negativa* is quite fundamental to a series of questions of major current significance for the future of the Christian tradition. These focus on the approach to be taken on the one hand to questions of a social and political nature and on the other to questions of the relationship between the major religious traditions of the world.

In a bold but admittedly potentially misleading way, I can summarize my view thus: theology's primary concern is with the possible. Such a claim even when clarified will make many feel uneasy, for, of course, in many contexts the possible is regarded as a diminution of the actual. Surely, it will be argued, what is only possibly true is of less significance than what is actually true, and what possibly exists is ontologically inferior to what actually or really exists. If I am to have any hope of dissolving such unease, I must set about clarifying the rather opaque claim that the primary concern of theology is the possible.

My first point is illustrative and suggestive rather than logically compelling. Consider the following passages from St Matthew's Gospel:

> The devil took him to a very high mountain, and showed him all the kingdoms of the world in their glory. 'All these', he said, 'I will give you, if you will only fall down and do me homage.' But Jesus said, 'Begone, Satan; Scripture says, "You shall do homage to the Lord your God and worship him alone." ' (4.8–10)

> He went on a little, fell on his face in prayer, and said, 'My Father, if it is possible, let this cup pass me by. Yet not as I will, but as thou wilt.' (26.39)

These two passages differ from each other in a number of ways. Each, however, apparently reports words said to, or by, a supernatural being. The point is this: why is it that we distinguish the first from the second by assuming that in the case of the first the question of whether an actual, real, supernatural being called Satan exists is not a relevant question to ask. The point of the story does not depend upon our first establishing or assuming that this is the report of a conversation between Jesus and an 'objectively' existing being. The religious or spiritual significance of the story does not depend upon a prior ontological commitment (although I do accept that for some it does – I merely disassociate myself from such a view). My question is (and for the moment we must remain with a question rather than an affirmation),

'Why should the theologian assume that the significance or truth of the second story depends any more than in the first case on the belief that there "actually", "objectively" exists a supernatural being who is hearing or uttering words?' For many this will be a shocking, because heretical question to raise, but I am not trying to persuade you that God does not actually, objectively exist; rather I am asking you to consider and perhaps reconsider what is meant in such a context either to claim that Satan does not *really* exist, or to claim that God does *actually* exist. I want, further, to ask whether shifting the emphasis here from actuality to possibility will help.

Let us turn to some more formal considerations about the difference between actuality and possibility. Consider the logical rule,

1 *ab esse ad posse valet consequentia.*

This logical rule, regarded by some as irreversible, encapsulates the picture of the relationship between the real and the possible which often dominates theological thinking including responses to the stories quoted from the first gospel. The primary application of the rule is of the form that if the present king of France really does exist, then it follows that it is possible that the present king of France exists, whereas if it is *only (sic)* possible that the present king of France exists, then it does not follow that he actually or really exists. The extension of this to the story of Gethsemane is as follows. If

(a) God the Father really does exist,
then it follows that
(b) it is possible that God the Father exists,
then it follows that
(c) it is possible that Jesus prayed as he did in Gethsemane and was not deluded.

The question raised by the story of the temptations is whether this implies that in order to accept

(c′) it is possible that Jesus fought temptation as he did in

the Wilderness, and was not deluded,
we must first accept

(a′) Satan really does exist?

I wish to reject the dependence of (c) on (a), just as I reject the
dependence of (c′) on (a′), not because I wish to negate (a),
but because I wish to substitute for logical rule 1,

2 *a posse ad esse valet consequentia.*

Now there are many caveats attached to this, but rather than
tediously list them all, I shall content myself with the most
important, and allow the rest to emerge in due course; I do
not wish to substitute 2 for 1 in all contexts. For example 1 is
clearly the correct rule to apply in empirical arguments. My
contention is that in *some* contexts 2 is a legitimate basis for
drawing inferences. Let me illustrate.

There is a limited comparison here with some aspects of
mathematics. Thus whereas it follows from

(d)   it is possible to prove Fermat's last theorem,
that
(e)   there is a proof of Fermat's last theorem,

it does not follow from

(d′) it is possible to build a fifty-storey green office block
      on the south bank of the Thames,
that
(e′) there is a fifty-storey green office block on the south
      bank of the Thames.

Or, a slightly different case, if it is possible to sum the
series $[1 + 1/2^x]$ where x is given the values from 1 to
infinity, then there *is* a sum of the infinite series in question.
In the cases just given, the inference from possibility to
actuality is valid. Of course the cases could be restructured
and restated in a number of ways which would invalidate the
inference, but my primary concern is to show that there are
cases of such valid inference.

It is important to note two central features of the second

case given. First, that there is a sum to infinity of that series does not depend upon there being a number which is that sum; second, the claim that there is such a sum depends upon its possibility in the sense of its intelligibility. From the intelligibility of the idea of a sum to infinity of that series we can validly draw the consequence that there is such a sum to infinity. Extending the idea a little further, if the idea of irrational numbers is intelligible, then there are irrational numbers, or approaching a little more closely to the central theme of this chapter, if, as Plato argued in the *Republic*, the idea of a just man is intelligible, then the reality of justice has been established. The two points which I want to insist on at this stage are that sometimes by showing that something is possible we can establish a sense in which it is actual; and also that the methods of enquiry appropriate in such an enterprise are conceptual rather than empirical.

I quite concede that the senses of the words, 'possible' and 'actual' are being stretched here. Indeed the stretching is deliberate, and if my point about the nature of theology is correct, then the pressure on these terms is necessary for the correct practice of the discipline.

If the primary concern of theology is with the possible, then, as is compatible with the approach followed in my discussion of moral and religious commitments in chapter 3, it is quite clear that theology is concerned directly with that men say and think and only indirectly with God. The possible here is to be understood as the limits of the intelligible – or the rational. The possibility of the life of faith is in this sense the intelligibility of the life of faith. This helps make our question clear and specific: is it possible that Jesus prayed as he did in Gethsemane and was not deluded? Is it possible that Jesus wrestled with temptation as he did in the wilderness and was not deluded? To answer these questions positively is to show how the claims implicit in such answers can be made intelligible.

Compare the analogous claims about Fermat's last theorem and Plato's just man. Is it possible that Fermat claimed that he had the proof in question and was not deluded? A positive answer must include showing that such a proof is possible. Is it possible that Socrates in the *Republic* could claim against Thrasymachus that there is justice and a just life, and not be deluded? A positive answer to that depends upon producing an argument comparable to that of the *Republic* which would defend the intelligibility of the idea. Despite the clear differences, which are partly logical in character, what these two cases have in common is that the answer in each case *is* the demonstration of the intelligibility of a series of connections and inferences between ideas. Theology has a great deal to learn from this, and much less to fear than might be first supposed. The approach which I am advocating is to examine the implications and intelligibility of claims such as that Jesus could pray as he did and not be deluded, and to establish the minimum conditions of the intelligibility of such claims and therefore of the possibility of the forms of religious faith which they define and exemplify. Theology, talk of God, will then be strictly limited to the role which it may have in elaborating these possibilities.

Undoubtedly such a role may have the appearance of parsimony – for some a further confirmation of the unfortunate consequence of admitting the philosophical Trojan horse into the theological camp. Such a judgment may be justified but not on the evidence so far. Consider two further general points.

In the proposed scheme what is being offered is a form of theological realism. Although the emphasis has been upon the possible and the intelligible, the conclusions have to do with the real and the actual. This can be shown in two ways. On the one hand I do want very firmly to draw the inference *a posse ad esse*. The conclusion has to do with how things are. That is to say the conclusions offered are conclusions about what the order of things will tolerate: what is possible is what the structures of reality allow as possible. On the other hand this can be shown by reference to the case of Jesus. My argument will be that it is possible that a man should so wrestle with temptation or pray and not be deluded. However, the possibility here is not 'psychological' or 'empirical' possibility (cf. Can I stand having dinner with the Fortescues again?), just as the possibility of a just man in the *Republic* does not have to do with weakness of will. To establish that religious faith or just living is possible in this context, is again to make affirmation about whether there is a real distinction between justice and injustice, or whether there is a *real* distinction between the temptations of evil and the inclinations of one's character or nature. To show the possibility, i.e. the intelligibility, of such distinctions is to show their reality or actuality.

The second general point which I wish to make starts from the reminder that theology has always beeen concerned with the limits of rationality and intelligibility. Aquinas, Calvin and Kierkegaard were all concerned with intellectual limits, and it is more common to quote than to give serious attention to Kant's confession: 'I have found it necessary to deny *knowledge*, in order to make room for *faith*.'[5] The temper of English-speaking philosophy under the influence of the Positivists and the earlier writings of Wittgenstein has inclined towards an interpretation of Kant which has placed emphasis upon the negative consequences of Kant's preoccupation with the limits of our understanding. (See, for example, the interesting final chapter of Stenius' book *Wittgenstein's 'Tractatus'*, 'Wittgenstein as a Kantian Philosopher',[6] or the title of P. F. Strawson's study of Kant, *The Bounds of Sense*.[7]) In recent philosophy the discussion of limits has focussed on the negative: what may not be thought; what may *not* be said; what is *not* intelligible and therefore not possible. The impetus of the present study lies in the *positive* converse of this, the establishing of what *is* possible, an the pattern of argument will be in terms of what is intelligible. Thus I am concerned to establish positively whether there is possible today a religious faith which neither distorts not ignores the structures of reality, and whether the language of theism has an essential role to play in this.

In the concluding pages of this chapter I shall begin to relate the comparatively theoretical isues which have been our concern to more specific questions about the content of such a theology.

In Robert Bolt's play *A Man for all Seasons* there is a scene in which Thomas More rejects Rich's request for advancement in the career of government and suggests to him that he should become a teacher. In response to Rich's implied suggestion that that isn't much of a job for a bright and ambitious young man, More tells Rich that if he becomes a teacher and teaches well, 'You will now it, your pupils will know it, and God will know it.' This example will help clarify the issues about possibility and theology which are my central concern.

The two fundamental theological questions which such an utterance provokes are:

(1) what is the difference between a man who adds, and means it, 'and God will know it', and a man who intentionally restricts himself to 'You will know it and your pupils will know it'?

(2) and is there any truth in the claim 'God will know it'?

One way of tackling these questions which I reject would run as follows: a man who asserts 'God will know it' is asserting that there actually is a supernatural being who knows all things and who will therefore know that Rich teaches well; his assertion is true if there really is such an omniscient being.

The main difficulty, which I see with that approach to theology is that it does not clearly distinguish between saying 'God will know it', and the following example suggested by Orwell's *1984*. Suppose on leaving prison Winston Smith had been advised to take up schoolteaching and told that if he teaches well, 'you will know it, your pupils will know it, and Big Brother will know it.' Someone who asserted that would be asserting that there really is someone who is (well-nigh) omniscient and who will therefore know whether Winston teaches well: his assertion would be true if there were such a person who knows if Winston teaches well.

My initial point is that from the suggestion 'Big Brother will know it' a whole series of implications flow which suggest that the implied parallelism of logical form between 'Big Brother will know it' and 'God will know it' is mistaken. For example, the whole force of Big Brother's claim depends upon the adequacy of this surveillance techniques, and the co-operation of most of the population as informers. It is also a claim which at some point or other may clearly be seen to be true or false. It makes sense, even if it turns out to be foolhardy, to suggest that Winston's actions might escape notice, or that if the whole population refuses to co-operate, things will change, and Big Brother will *not* know it. In the case of 'God will know it', none of the parallel implications follow. There is no dependence on surveillance techniques; God does not 'notice' or 'come to know' things; he does not depend on informers; and there is nothing which human beings can do which will detract from or alter the truth of the claim 'and God will know it'.

The original question therefore still stands: what is the difference between the man who asserts 'God will know it', and the man who refuses to assert this, or alternatively the policeman who says 'Big Brother will know it'?

The suggestion which I offer is that we obscure rather than clarify these crucial differences if we *begin* by affirming that it has to do with an omniscient God who really or actually exists. Let us begin rather by looking at the affirmations which might follow 'God will know it'. Whereas after 'Big Brother will know it', what we can envisage is 'and so you'd better take care', or some equivalent, in the case of More's advice to Rich, a theatre critic who asked why More did not underline his point by appeal to his own undeniable power as Lord Chancellor, would betray a complete misunderstanding on what had been said. The same applies to a theological back-woodsman who claimed that More was *threatening* Rich with the activities of a Celestial Intelligence Agency. Quite to the contrary, the sorts of comments which we can imagine being added to More's 'and God will know it' are of the sort: '. . . and what else would a man want', or '. . . and won't that be enough to satisfy any man'.

No I must immediately insist that I am not translating 'and

God will know it' into either of these additional expressions, and I realize that I will have to confront the issue of reductionism in due course. My proposal at present is rather that we should consider these additional comments as clues to the meaning of 'and God will know it': they are clues to the procedure we must follow if we are to begin theological reflection on the idea of the omniscience of God.

To add 'and God will know it' is to talk about possibilities: in this example it is to affirm certain possibilities about human fulfilment and human self-knowledge, but, I insist, it is not simply to translate one set of terms into another. The man who affirms 'God will know it', in this case More, is *in part* affirming what Rich denies: namely that certain kinds of fulfilment are possible. Certain qualifications and additions must immediately be noted. First, the fulfilment in question has a very specific character to which certain values are non-contingently related. Second, More is also affirming that it may well not even occur to Rich to deny let alone affirm, namely that a man may know himself thoroughly and that the consequent transparency to himself and to others is again non-contingently related to the fulfilment in question. There is a third dimension to More's conception of what is possible which is certainly not dreamt of in Rich's world, to which we shall return in due course.

A fairly standard, but illuminating response to the suggestion which I am making is that to argue for such an account of 'and God will know it', is to produce a rather stunted or anaemic account of what *prima facie* purports to be a grand and informative statement about the way things are. Let me consider first the implication that More's affirmation about the possibilities of human self-fulfilment is rather small beer. I should want to argue that, quite to the contrary, if More is correct, then it is difficult to imagine a more important claim – this is a view I share with the writer of Ecclesiastes:

> I applied my mind to seek and to search out by wisdom all that is done under heaven; it is an unhappy business that God has given to the sons of men to be busy with. I have seen everything that is done under the sun; and behold all is vanity and a striving after wind. (1.13)

I hold no brief for the view that the claim that fulfilment can be found in human life is of limited importance.

Further, I do believe that there is a confusion implicit in the suggestion that my account of 'and God will know it' some-how is avoiding the important questions of the structures of being, or of the fundamental questions of ontology. We unduly limit ourselves if we regard our ontology as being defined by the list of things and types of things that there actually are. In some ways, *what is possible* has an even more significant role to play in the definition of our world or, if you prefer it, of our ontology. Let me put the point in this way: there is an *ontological* difference between a world in which fulfilment can be found in human life, and one in which this is not so. Between the man whose final word is 'Vanity of vanities, all is vanity' and More who can say to Rich 'You will know it, or your pupils will know it, and God will know it,' there is not simply a difference in attitude, there is a difference in ontology. The *possibilities* defined by the structures of their respective worlds are radically different, and in the end that is a difference about the way things are. In certain contexts (and this is one of them) possibilities define ontologies *a posse ad esse valet consequentia.*

6

Sub Specie Aeternitatis I

In the last chapter the first steps were taken in offering a sketch of a view summed up in the claim that theology's primary concern is with the possible. Points of comparison were suggested between the manner in which theology should be concerned to establish possibilities and what it would be to show that Fermat was correct in his claim that he had a proof for 'Fermat's last theorem', and what it would be to answer Thrasymachus' question about the nature of the just other than in his own reductionist claims that the 'just is nothing else than the advantage of the stronger'. Theology, it was implied, should be concerned primarily to examine claims such as that Jesus wrestled with temptation or prayed as he did in Gethsamane and was not deluded. If claims such as these could be established, then theology would have demonstrated the reality of what I take to be its central claim. The formulation of that claim must wait for a moment until we remind ourselves of the significance of the words which Bolt's Thomas More utters to Rich: 'You will know it; your pupils will know it; and God will know it.' The first question to ask is this: What further possibility is More intending when he adds the words, 'and God will know it'?

The answer to that must have at least two elements to it: on the one hand More must be alluding to a possible way of understanding oneself and one's place in the word in which one lives; on the other he must also be alluding to a correlated way of living in that world. The central question can now be formulated: what can be said to counter the claim that More was dealing in fantasies or delusions? My answer must be stated in the terms outlined in the last chapter: if we are to avoid the charge of fantasy and delusion, and show that we are dealing with reality, it must be by establishing the possibility, understood as 'intelligibility', of the viewpoint in question. Let us see how far we can go towards this.

It is interesting and significant that Bolt has given to More the language of theism ('*God* will know it') to do this. My fundamental claim will be that the language of theism is particularly well placed to perform this task, and the role of theology understood as a form of a natural religion is to examine why and how this is so. The answer to these questions is that the language of theism embodies, offers and protects the possibility of a view of human affairs *sub specie aeternitatis*. Further it raises the question which I believe it to be the task of philosophy (*vis-à-vis* theology) to answer: How, if at all, can the claim that this view represents the truth of the matter be elaborated and defended?

There are two jewels which lie at the heart of the possibility of a view *sub specie aeternitatis*: The first defines the hope, and indeed the belief, that there is an understanding of the affairs of men which is not relative to the outlook of individual, community or age. The second, which crowns that, is the implication that such a view is not even relative to the outlook of mankind. It is not in the language of today, even species relative, and therefore cannot be dismissed as anthropocentric. The only way of showing such a view to be anthropocentric would be to show that it was not truly '*sub specie aeternitatis*', but was simply a product of human hopes or fears projected outwards. Basically there are two ways of establishing such a conclusion. One is to show that the 'content' of the alleged view, when examined, gives the lie to the claim that it is *aeternitatis*: the other is to discredit the possibility of a view *sub specie aeternitatis* altogether, by showing it either formally to contain a contradiction, or to be unintelligible. My argument is in principle vulnerable to the latter strategy, but not equally so to the former. My protection against the former will be an extreme reticence to define what the 'content' of a view *sub specie aeternitatis* is. I believe that good grounds can be given for such reticence. Initially, however, it can be claimed that the possibility of a view *sub specie aeternitatis* which represents the truth of how things are rather than the limited and relative outlook of the temporal human understanding. Logically the appropriate procedure is to *exemplify* rather than *define* such a view. The reasons for this will emerge.

The dangers in such an idea are of course profound, and careful thinkers have adopted a variety of ways of warning us against them. St Paul warned us that we do but 'see through a glass darkly' and Kierkegaard, typically, poured scorn on the idea when he asked of the 'unworldly' philosopher: 'Is he himself *sub specie aeternitatis*, even when he sleeps, eats, blows his nose, or whatever else a philsopher does?' These warnings, however, are not directly relevant, for they presuppose that our hope is to attain the viewpoint of eternity, to see, in anthropomorphic terms, how and what *God* sees. I have already (chapters 2 and 4) given grounds for regarding such a picture as unacceptable. More significantly at this stage, it is important to distinguish between postulating a view *sub specie aeternitatis* and postulating the attainment of the viewpoint of God.

My argument is this: the possibility of a view *sub specie aeternitatis* is perculiarly well marked out in the language of theism. Indeed I should go as far as arguing that it is the non-anthropomorphic understanding of that language. The possibility of such a view *is* the possibility of living as More recommends Rich to live without being deluded. It also *is*, in ways that require a much more detailed elaboration than it is possible to give here, the possibility of fighting temptation or praying as Jesus did, without being deluded. There is here, however, a residual ambiguity in the notion of a view *sub specie aeternitatis* which we ought to clear up now. This expression could refer to one of two different options:

(1) the position from which one views the world – from eternity;

(2) *what* one sees, how the world is seen, when viewed *sub specie aeternitatis*.

We can never reach (1). This is not simply because we are finite and temporal but because the notion of a viewpoint understood in terms of (1) which is eternal is at most (for all the reasons elaborated in chapter 4) a confused and confusing metaphor, i.e. the notion is not intelligible. The idea contained in (2), however, is intelligible, for it refers to a possible way of understanding the world which has correlated to it a way of living in the world. There is still great difficulty in claiming that any one of us has or will ever attain that view, but the reasons for this are quite different. The difference can be brought out in this way: whereas the difficulty of reaching (1) is the difficulty of adopting the viewpoint of a traditional anthropomorphic God, the difficulty of attaining (2) is the difficulty of claiming that Jesus was in some sense divine. The questions raised by this account of (2) will be given fuller treatment in chapters 8–12.

At best we can approximate to such a view of ourselves and our world, but what is crucial, as we shall see, is the belief in the possibility of such a view. We can, however, only approximate, for those who remind us of our historicity, of our cultural anchorings, of our limitations psychological, social and epistemological, are right to do so. But what they cannot legitimately do is *on the same grounds* rule out the possibility of a view *sub specie aeternitatis*. They can only concur in the judgement of Christian theology that we are limited and finite creatures who 'see through a glass darkly'. Indeed an awareness of this limitation is essential to my case.

The limitations is not, however, comparable to the limitation which leads Hick to give an account of religious faith in terms of 'experiencing as'. His case is based upon stressing purely the epistemological limitations to which we are subject and which are typical of *all* forms of experiencing. He regards faith 'as the interpretative element within our cognitive religious experience.[1] Certainly the idea of a view '*sub specie aeternitatis*' stresses also the importance of interpretation, but the underlying model in Hick's account is quite different. He is operating within the basic pattern of empirical enquiry in which from the date of one's experience one constructs an interpretation which will allow one to make inferences about the existence of God who lies beyond our experience. The view of which I speak is one which is ultimately judged, not as in Hick's case on its plausibility, but on its intelligibility. Thus whereas a man might admit of a puzzle picture. 'Yes although I see it as a duck, I do see that it can be taken as a rabbit,' the possibilities to which I refer are ultimately either intelligible or unintelligible. The structures of reality either tolerate such a possibility or they do not. Thus when reference is made to the possibility of a view *sub specie aeternitatis*, the possibility being spoken of is more in Kantian than *gestalt* or empirical terms. The relations can then be understood as follows: the condition of the possibility of a non-deluded form of life such as More advocated to Rich, or of the possibility of non-deluded wrestling with temptation or prayer as in the case of Jesus, is the possibility of a view *sub specia aeternitatis* of the affairs of men. However, whether such a view is possible cannot be spoken of *per se*, as it were, by describing the viewpoint independently of the form of life of which it is the condition. The relationship between the two is non-contingent, and the viewpoint cannot be individuated and described (as in (1) above) independently of the way of understanding and living of which it is the condition. This is complex, but not as logically unique or extraordinary as it might seem.

Consider an example to which reference has already been made:

$$\int_\infty^1 (1 + 1/2^x) = 1 + \frac{1}{2} + \frac{1}{4} + \ldots$$

Now the possibility of there being a sum of the series on the right-hand side of the equation depends upon the condition that there is such a thing as a 'sum to infinity', but if we use that point as an argument for insisting on an account of the left-hand side of the equation independently of the right-hand side, we shall be guilty of a misunderstanding. But this does not make this formula and this equation trivial, for the way of thinking implied in the idea of a sum to infinity, in the idea of seeing the right-hand side *as a series* extends our conceptual abilities and *ipso facto* our ability to grasp features of our world which would otherwise not be available to us. To adapt a remark from the previous chapter, there is a difference between a man who can use the expression 'sum to infinity' and one who cannot, and the difference shows in the range of interactions with the world open to the one and not to the other. There is also a sense in which it is true that the difference between the two men is a difference about how it is possible to construe the series $1 + \frac{1}{2} + \frac{1}{4} + \frac{1}{8} \ldots$, and that a condition of construing it in the one way rather than the other is the possibility of there being a sum to infinity. The crucial point for us is the meaning of such a claim.

I wish to suggest a parallel between this case and the case under discussion, viz. the relation between a view *sub specie aeternitatis* and the way in which we see the world. My argument is that the language of theism has been the way in which in our culture, and others, this view has been preserved and articulated. However, it would be easy for me to underestimate the problems inherent in the claim which I am making, and I want to exorcise some of these by considering some alternative attempts to characterize a view *sub specie aeternitatis*.

As has already been made plain, it is important to distinguish between the sense of this expression which implies, in terms of some quasi-spatial metaphor, that there is a place from which such a viewpoint is obtained, and one which denies this. The former possibility, which I have already given grounds for rejecting, is theistically associated with the idea of seeing the world as or from the place where God sees it. A condition of making this metaphor intelligible is the resolution of the problems set out in chapters 2 and 4. I do not propose to discuss this further at present.

All philosophers who have written about eternity are difficult, but in some cases one gains the impression – usually no more than that – of profundity. Spinoza belongs to this latter group. Yet when we turn to his words, we cannot but agree with Wisdom's conclusion:

> Spinoza's words when he says that we feel and know that we are eternal, and when he speaks of seeing things under a species of eternity, may linger in one's mind even after one has been driven to admit that what he says by way of indicating what he means has left one still at a loss as to what he means and, perhaps, with a suspicion that he himself is not clear as to what he means.[2]

Although this following passage is not the one to which he gives a reference, it is clear that it exemplifies the type of remark in question:

> Eternity is the essence of God in so far as this necessarily involves existence (Def 8, Part I). Therefore to conceive things under the species of eternity is to conceive them in so far as they are conceived through the essence of God as real entities, or in so far as they involve existence through the essence of God. And therefore our mind, in so far as it conceives itself and its body under a species of eternity, has thus far necessarily a knowledge of God . . .'[3]

In his attempt to make what sense he can of this elusive sense of the eternal, Wisdom refers to the case of Dr Bucke, discussed by both William James and W. T. Stace.

The emphasis in the example of Bucke is upon a moment of insight or illumination which in some sense at least is intended to represent the consciousness of the eternal – an insight for some which would be the condition of legitimately laying claim to a viewpoint on the world *sub specie aeternitatis*. I am making explicit such a view in order to reject it. The quotation from Bucke offered by James is as follows:

> I had spent the evening in a great city, with two friends, reading and discussing poetry and philosophy. We parted at midnight. I had a long drive in a hansom to my lodging. My mind, deeply under the influence of the ideas, images, and emotions called up by the reading and talk, was calm and peaceful. I was in a state of quiet, almost passive enjoyment,

not actually thinking, but letting ideas, images, and emotions flow of themselves, as it were, through my mind. All at once, without warning of any kind, I found myself wrapped in a flame-coloured cloud. For an instant I thought of fire, an immense conflagration somewhere close by in that great city; the next, I knew that the fire was within myself. Directly afterwards there came upon me a sense of exultation, of immense joyousness accompanied or immediately followed by an intellectual illumination impossible to describe. Among other things, I did not merely come to believe, but I saw that the universe is not composed of dead matter, but is, on the contrary, a living Presence; I became conscious in myself of eternal life. It was not a conviction that I would have eternal life, but a consciousness that I possessed eternal life then; I saw that all men are immortal; that the cosmic order is such that without any peradventure all things work together for the good of each and all; that the foundation principle of the world, of all the worlds, is what we call love, and that the happiness of each and all is in the long run absolutely certain. The vision lasted a few seconds and was gone but the memory of it and the sense of the reality of what it taught have remained during the quarter of a century which has since lapsed. I knew that what the vision showed was true. I had attained to a point of view from which I saw that it must be true. That view, that conviction, I may say that consciousness, has never, even during periods of the deepest depression, been lost.[4]

Now whatever the circumstances described, the possibility of the appeal to such an experience lies behind many discussions of eternity. I do not wish to discuss the details of this or other cases, for appeal to such unusual experiences is no part of my case. I must admit, however, that where I have examined accounts of such experiences, they do seem to promise more than they can sustain. There is already an extensive literature on the attempt to use a subjective experience or moment of apparent vision in order to validate a claim of a particular interpretation of experience to be a view of the world *sub specie aeternitatis*. The result of that discussion does seem to me to show that however striking or indeed important such experiences are, their primary significance is not epistemological. For my purposes this does not matter, for I do not wish to validate a particular view or vision by claiming some special experiential or revelatory status for it. Indeed such a possibility seems to me not to be compatible with the stance of natural religion.

There are, however, more subtle and indeed wistful ways of invoking some analogue of this. In her quite remarkable and stimulating essay, 'On "God" and "Good"', Iris Murdoch writes, 'I shall suggest that God was (or is) a *single perfect transcendent non-representable and necessarily real object of attention*; and I shall go on to suggest that moral philosophy should attempt to retain a central concept which has all these characteristics.'[5] There is much in this essay with which I am in total agreement, but the difficulty of the issues under consideration inevitably leaves patches of shade where what is being thought and said is far from clear. The idea of the transcendent shies away from the notions of the single, and what is an *object* of attention. The problems inherent in this combination of ideas are plain in the following reflection on Plato, in which Miss Murdoch relies on a series of metaphors which do not give unity to her account:

> The Good is not visible. Plato pictured the good man as eventually able to look at the sun. I have never been sure what to make of this part of the myth. While it seems proper to represent the Good as a centre or focus of attention, yet it cannot be experienced or represented or defined. We can certainly know more or less where the sun is; it is not so easy to imagine what it would be like to look at it. Perhaps only the good man knows what this is like; or perhaps to look at the sun is to be gloriously dazzled and to see nothing. What does seem to make perfect sense in the Platonic myth is the idea of the Good as the source of light which reveals to us all things as they really are. (p. 70)

One major and crucial difference between what is said here and the approach of Bucke is that the idea of the Good as an object of attention or of 'seeing the sun' is not offered as providing an epistemological basis or justification for a particular interpretation or experience.

None the less the hesitancy shown over what is in some sense the culmination of the Platonic myth – looking at the sun – should give cause for reflection. The problems involved were grasped by Plato in a number of the dialogues, but most clearly in the *Sophist*. At the heart of the matter is the question of whether the forms, including the Good, can be spoken of as particulars. This is not the moment to rehearse the literature on this point, but the issue of particularity is central to the present discussion. In the fourth chapter I attributed many of the difficulties of traditional theism to the view that God is an individual. In the passage quoted above, Miss Murdoch is partly, but not completely, acknowledging that there are similar problems for the idea of the Good. The issue of goodness and particularity will be the subject of an extended discussion in a later chapter, but one point must be made here.

Despite the various *caveats* and qualifications, there is a clear sense in which Miss Murdoch wishes to regard the transcendent Good as an object of attention. This is to regard it as in some sense a particular. The reasons for rejecting this view are parallel to my reasons for rejecting the view of God as an individual. Against these, it is possible to offer a number of possible defences or elaborations of view. On the one hand she is very conscious of the powerful effect of prayer as a means of intellectual and moral purification. However, she cannot consistently, nor, I suspect, would she, offer this as adequate grounds for particularizing the Good: she is very firm in rejection of the consolatory powers of a belief as good reason for accepting it. Surely she must be equally firm in using the *effectiveness* of the idea of an object of prayer/ attention as grounds for an ontological claim if that effectiveness is understood even partially in causal terms. My point here is that the justification for retaining the idea of a transcendent Good must lie not in what it *does*, but in the vision to which it gives rise. If the relationship between transcendent Good and vision is contingent, then why retain the idea as more or less than the occasion of insight. As Kierkegaard pointed out, occasions, like teachers, are quite dispensible: it is the lesson learned which counts. If, however, the relationship between the idea of the Good and vision of the world (*sub specie aeternitatis*) to which it gives rise is non-contingent, then the force for insisting upon the Good as an object of attention is spent. The question of whether God, or the Good, is correctly presented as an individual, even in the limited sense of a possible object of prayer or attention, is a question of the truth of this representation rather than its effectiveness.

Miss Murdoch has clearly been influenced by the writings of Simone Weil, and it is most likely that her stress upon the idea of attention owes much to Miss Weil. In this respect, however, she does differ in emphasis from Weil, for although Weil attaches great significance to the idea of attention, she does so in the context of the attention which we give to other people, their needs, their sorrows, their happiness, rather than regarding 'the Good' as an object of attention. In this I prefer Weil: attention as in the parable of the good Samaritan is to be given to the particular and limited. Transcendent Good is not thus a possible object of attention. Indeed the point of the parable suggests that the very idea may be a distraction. I do confess here to a selective emphasis upon elements of Iris Murdoch's essay, but these are the elements which distract from much that is important and profound.

A further point of difference between the views being offered here and Miss Murdoch's position is the limited but important place which she gives to the idea of certainty.

> I think the idea of transcedence here connects with two separate ideas . . .: *perfection* and *certainty*. Are we not certain that there is a 'true direction' towards better conduct, that goodness 'really matters', and does not that certainty about a standard suggest an idea of permanence which cannot be reduced to psychological or any other set of empirical terms? (ibid., p. 60)

My answer to this rhetorical question is 'Yes and No'. The finitude and agnosticism which I have stressed in relation to the idea of God applies also to the idea of the Good. This most clearly lies behind the reluctance shown in this chapter to accept any claim, even in the muted form offered by Miss Murdoch that behind the idea of a view of the world *sub specie aeternitatis* lies a transcendent or eternal something with which we may have a relationship ('awareness', 'vision', 'seeing') which is other than the relationship which we have to the world viewed *sub specie aeternitatis*, but as the contortions and complexities of the argument of this chapter must have demonstrated, we can give an account of this only with great patience and care. In the next chapter I hope to unravel the knot a little further.

It might help clarify matters if I relate these very abstract arguments to the examples given in the last chapter. Thomas More recommends to Rich a way of living which is clearly different from what Rich had in mind. In Gethsemane Jesus, in prayer, prepares himself for the death which will capture, in essence, a way of living. The death, and *ipso facto* the life, was not what the disciples hoped and planned for Jesus or for themselves. In the wilderness Jesus wrestles with temptation in a manner which implies that he wrestles with what is real, rather than with elements of his own pathology. In each of these cases the possibility that what is done or recommended is other than a product of fantasy or dream, depends, I am suggesting, on the idea of a particular view of the world and of the affairs of men – that view is of the world *sub specie aeternitatis*. This is a view of the world neither shared nor aspired to by Rich, and certainly not fully understood by the disciples.

Yet it is not a view to be attained by trying to see the world 'as God sees it', from eternity. Nor again is it a view that depends upon the sort of experience or 'brush with eternity' described by Bucke. Even the much more careful suggestion by Murdoch that we make central to such a view the postulation of 'a *single perfect transcendent non-representable and necessarily real object of attention*', is not an acceptable approach to the intelligibility of a view of the world *sub specie aeternitatis*. For Rich to see the world as More sees it, what is required is not to attend to such a transcendent object as 'the Good', but to attend to the needs of others and the character of his own ambition.

Thus view of the world *sub specie aeternitatis* is nothing-more nor less than a view of the world; it is how the world is seen when it is seen *sub specie aeternitatis*. It is not something other than the world seen and experienced. To postulate such a view is to talk about how it is possible to understand the world and to live in it.

7

Sub Specie Aeternitatis II

In the last two chapters I have been arguing that the legacy of the language and thought of theism is an awareness of the possibility which is encapsulated in a view of the world *sub specie aeternitatis*. So far the content of such a view has not been elaborated in any detail and there are many reasons for this. The most important of these is that elaborating a view of the world *sub specie aeternitatis*, if it is possible at all, cannot be just like elaborating any other view of the world. For example, the world viewed under the aspect of economic development, or of the maximization of pleasure, or of the political supremacy of this race or that, or even of distributing material benefit as equally as possible, in each case is the world understood under some limited and, to that extent, manageable aspect. There is a risk that the notion of a world view *sub specie aeternitatis* leaves us exactly where we begin – lacking firm guidelines as to how we may set about elaborating such a view, for to elaborate is to select, and to select is to be particular and exclude, but what does the aspect of *eternity* exclude? How can the aspect of eternity take *particular* shape?

Frustratingly perhaps, I must postpone answering that question until the next chapter, for the groundwork necessary to an adequate appreciation of it must be laid in this. None the less, some pointers have been given in terms of the stories of Jesus' temptation, and his prayer in Gethsemane; equally the words of Robert Bolt's Thomas More to Rich, 'You will know it, your pupils will know it, and God will know it', have served to raise the question of the significance which we might attach to the addition of the last five words. These examples will help us clarify the next stage of the argument. The questions which they raise have particular form. Is it possible that Jesus prayed or wrestled with temptation as he did and was not deluded? Could Rich have replied by accusing More of deceiving himself by imagining that what God might or might not know could have anything to do with the matter at all? In more general terms, the idea of a view *sub specie aeternitatis* ostensively defined in these examples is vulnerable to attack from two different directions. On the one hand the Richs of this world might pour scorn on such an idea at all and argue that More, or for that matter Jesus, offers us simply an alternative relative view of the world, subject to the determinants of time and psyche. Such a response suggests the relativist sceptical option which would deny that a view *sub specie aeternitatis* is possible at all. On the other hand the traditional theist may attack from the opposite end of the spectrum by arguing that in essence my analysis of theism understood as the possibility of a view *sub specie aeternitatis* is reductionist: that in place of belief in a transcendent objective being I am offering a mess of reductionist pottage – a subjective account of how the world might, as it so happens, be seen. Each of these attacks complements the other and this is not surprising, for a marked and continuing feature of the discussion of religious belief has been a series of strange alliances between theological traditionalists and sceptics. Defence against the one set of questions may often serve as protection against the other.

The suggestions that Rich or Jesus may simply be offering a further relative way of seeing things must be countered in two ways. One, which must be postponed, will require detailed discussion of the nature of the values implicit in what they say and do: a second concerns the radical proposal that a non-relative view or a view *sub specie aeternitatis* is not intelligible and in that sense not possible. If this is true, then to echo the words of St Paul, 'we are of all men the most miserable'.

The first point of response is that we must draw a distinction between two senses of 'possibility'. It is one thing to argue that no human being is capable of so escaping from the bonds of finitude that he might view the world *sub specie aeternitatis*; it is quite another to argue that the idea of such a perspective is unintelligible. In the former sense – of capacity or ability – the notion of a view *sub specie aeternitatis* may not be possible for us, while the idea of such a view might itself be quite intelligible and, in this second sense, possible.

The position which I am defending is not committed to the claim that any individual can slough off the constraints of finitude. If the argument of the sceptic rests on the premiss that I am proposing that human beings may aspire to (traditionally) where God stands, then it fails. There is no attempt to aspire to superhumanity, to see 'as God sees'. Nor is it implied that in seeking to view the world *sub specie aeternitatis*, we must first seek the vantage point of eternity. There is no technique, not even the Platonic, for seeing either 'from' or 'into' eternity. Likewise, to see the world *sub specie aeternitatis* is not to glimpse something called 'the eternal' or 'the transcendent'. It is to see the world, and to respond to that world *sub specie aeternitatis*. The eternal, the transcendent is not a *feature* or an *aspect* of the world. It is a possibility contained within the structures of the world. It is a possibility which can be recognized, as in the case of More, or one which can be rejected as Rich did. But its recognition does not presuppose a non-finite viewpoint, nor a non-finite or transcendent object to be discerned or glimpsed.

What is crucial in all this, is that in order to make the best of our limited perceptions, in order to be least misled by the finitude of our experience, we must think and perceive and act in a world which contains the possibility of being viewed *sub specie aeternitatis*. Herein lie the ontological implications of my view, for a world which tolerates that possibility, a world in which that possibility is intelligible, is a world far different from one which is structured to admit only of the relative shifting and the finite. I shall return to this point.

Two more pressing questions must preoccupy us now.

What difference does it make to affirm the intelligibility of the notion of a view of the world *sub specie aeternitatis* – especially if that is a view to which, at best, we approximate? Further, is there any basis for accepting the legitimacy of such a claim?

There is an analogy between the role which I am assigning to the idea of a view *sub specie aeternitatis*, and the role which Kant assigns to what he calls the 'transcendental ideas' of reason: he writes,

> I accordingly maintain that transcendental ideas never allow of any constitutive employment. When regarded in that mistaken manner, and therefore as supplying concepts of certain objects, they are but pseudo-rational, merely dialectical concepts. On the other hand, they have an excellent, and indeed indispensably necessary, regulative employment, namely that of directing the understanding towards a certain goal upon which the routes marked out by all its rules converge, as upon their point of intersection. This point is a mere idea, a *focus imaginarius*, from which since it lies quite outside the bounds of possible experience, the concepts of the understanding do not in reality proceed.[1]

Now there are also disanalogies, for Kant goes on to talk of 'illusion' here, and for various reasons which will emerge I am very reluctant to do this. However, Kant did see both the importance of, and the difficulty in characterizing, the role of Regulative Ideas.

There are two elements of Kant's attachment to Regulative Ideas upon which we might focus briefly. The first is that negatively their role in Kant's philosophy is an elaboration of the strongly agnostic element in *Critique of Pure Reason*. Without doubt he sets severe limits both to what we do know and what we may know. His 'agnosticism' has the special character of limitations to knowledge being set by the limitations of intelligibility. This carries it far beyond the agnosticism which is the product of the empiricist's awareness of the perhaps temporary or relative limits to what as a matter of fact we can now justifiably claim to know. I am in total sympathy with the Kantian stress on the importance of the limits of intelligibility. As Kant applies these to the problems of the role of the concept of God, and even of the word 'God', so I apply them to the idea of a view 'sub specie aeternitatis'.

"However there is a second feature of Kant's thought here (or at least of how we in the second half of the twentieth century are inclined to interpret him) which I mention in order to disassociate myself from it. In the vigour of his attack on false and speculative metaphysics Kant often seems to want to take no ontological responsibility whatsoever for his use of Regulative Ideas: '. . . never allow of any constitutive employment . . .'; '. . . a mere idea of a focus imaginarius, from which . . . the concepts of the understanding do not in reality proceed'. However, there is no question of my contradicting Kant – and indeed what I have argued in previous chapters – by insisting that we must reinstate the concept of God as a constitutive concept which derives its sense from the fact that there is such a being, albeit 'quite outside the bounds of possible experience'. I accept that Kant finally closed the door to that pattern or argument. None the less, in doing so he did not, for he could not, disqualify all metaphysical or ontological questions. We can still ask of Kant, as of any other philosopher or theologian, 'What must the world be like if Kant's account of our knowledge of it is correct?'

Here we must draw a number of distinctions, the first of which was canvassed in the fifth chapter. Theologies, it was suggested, might be roughly characterized according to whether their nucleus was a series of affirmations about God, or about the World, or about Self. The characterization can easily become caricature, but it does indicate absolutely crucial differences of emphasis. The door which I believe Kant has closed is the door to a theology which belongs to the first area of emphasis – a theology which I agree has been the dominant form – one which is first and last concerned to make affirmations about an individual being who transcends the world. A pattern of argument which remains open is for a theology which is in the end concerned to characterize the world. Whether the resultant theology is reductionist cannot be prejudged: it depends upn the characterization of the world which is offered. One point about which we can be very clear is that the characterization in question cannot shun ontological implications.

The notion of 'the world' at play here can be understood in a number of ways. At the beginning of the *Tractatus*,[2] Wittgenstein offered the following definitions:

1.   The world is all that is the case.
1.1 The world is the totality of facts, not of things.

These definitions and his explication of them have the merit of reminding us that 'the world' need not be construed as 'the empirical world of the senses'. Neither in themselves, however, nor in the light of the connotations which they now carry for all philosophers, can they serve our present purposes. The first may be incorporated into my text as it stands, but the second must be rephrased.

1.1a The world is the totality of possibilities, not of things.

The philosophical ramifications are immense, but the new formula simultaneously detaches our concerns from those of the *Tractatus*, and indicates why I argue that the possible is the key to the real.

Although Kant never believed, as Vaihinger appeared to do, that one could use pragmatic arguments to provide a justification for the widespread use of ideas whose epistemological and metaphysical status is otherwise suspect, it is clear that the plausibility of his very limited appeal to Regulative Ideas depends in part on the fact that we do think according to certain patterns and not others. I would make a claim of an analogously limited kind in offering a plausibility argument in support of the idea of a view *sub specie aeternitatis*. In this I am once again helped by Murdoch's exploration of related questions in *The Sovereignty of Good*. She is dealing with the sense which can be attached to the idea of 'a *single perfect transcendent non-representable and necessarily real object of attention*' (p. 55), as the idea might have significance for moral philosophy. Yet much of what she writes, the qualifications as well as the assertions, has relevance for the idea of a view *sub specie aeternitatis*.

There is, she suggests, at least psychological force in the belief 'in the unity and also in the hierarchical order of the moral world' (p. 56). Of more than psychological significance is the fact that the intellect, 'naturally seeks unity; and in the sciences, for instance, the assumption of unity consistently rewards the seeker . . .' (p. 56). And on the moral front, 'reflection rightly tends to unify the moral world, and . . . increasing moral sophistication reveals increasing unity' (p. 57). An important, indeed constitutive element of thought about 'any field which concerns or interests us' (p. 61) is the measuring and comparing of things on a scale whose end point is, in principle, perfection, in order to 'know just how good they are'. 'The idea of perfection works thus within a field of study, producing an increasing sense of direction.' (pp. 61–2) Each of these points can have application, if necessary by rephrasing, to the idea of a view *sub specie aeternitatis*. Equally the notion of such a view gains in plausibility as we see how our understanding of, and response to, the world presupposes something of the sort. This point can be most clearly appreciated from its negative aspect: in a world in which all *possible* views were relative and limited, there would be no sense in the idea of a hierarchy in the moral world, or in the idea of a measuring and comparing in respect of quality or goodness; indeed we would be inclined to see the rewards of, as well as the search for unity in, the world of science as having nothing to do with truth and reality.

However, as Murdoch stresses, there are dangers in such a pattern of thought – not least in theism where 'As soon as any idea is a consolation the tendency to falsify it becomes strong: hence the traditional problem of preventing the idea of God from degenerating in the believer's mind' (p. 57). There are comparable dangers for someone outside the mainstream of theism for there 'a reductionist might argue that an increasingly refined ability to compare need not imply anything beyond itself. The idea of perfection might be, as it were, empty' (p. 62). Equally, it might be said, the reductionist could argue that my account of the content of theism in terms of the possibility of a view *sub specie aeternitatis* is a confession of the emptiness of a tradition which once boasted distinctive ontological commitments. This charge of reductionism which has shadowed my argument throughout must now be confronted.

Despite my affirmations to the contrary, it may well still seem that in the end I am offering a reductionist account of belief in God. For example, in relation to the apparent reference by More to God's omniscience – 'and God will know it' – I write of the possibility of complete fulfilment in human life. Likewise, I confess that if I were to begin to tease out the meaning of the stories of the temptation of Jesus, and of the prayers of Jesus in Gethsemane, I would do so respectively in terms of the possibilities defined by a temptation which might win the soul (a theme treated with great insight by Marlowe, Goethe, Mann, etc.), and the possibilities of complete self-giving ('not my will . . .') in the face of all that would distract us from it. These stories make affirmations about our world because they affirm what is possible in it. However, it might be asked, can these possibilities not be equally well defined without *any* reference to God, without *any* hint of religious belief? Indeed, in my paraphrases have I not done precisely this?

And so we return to our two earlier questions:

(1) what is the difference between a man who adds, and means it, 'and God will know it', and a man who intentionally restricts himself to 'You will know it, and your pupils will know it'?

(2) and is there any truth in the claim 'God will know it'?

Suppose that a man does find life fulfilled in the way More implies; or, to reintroduce the two earlier examples, suppose a man goes through a Gethsemane type experience, or through a temptation of fire, as for example the temptation to seek power so vividly portrayed in the gospel stories of

Jesus' temptations: in each of these cases we must be able to make intelligible the distinction between the moral hero and the fanatic, or between the saintly and the insane. It would be easy to give many examples of cases where if someone adopts a morally heroic posture, the question of either fanaticism or insanity must at least be asked. Literature provides many such cases each worthy of quite separate analysis: for example Sarah, the heroine in Graham Greene's *The End of the Affair;* Alissa in Gide's *Strait is the Gate*, the prince in Tolstoy's *Resurrection*, Brand in Ibsen's play, and so on.[3] Each is a classic example of a case where moral heroism may be apparent rather than real – a sign of fanaticism or insanity rather than sainthood.

As the administrative genius who devised the infamous Catch-22 ruling of Heller's novel saw all too clearly, one of the most crucial signs of sanity is the awareness of the need to draw a distinction between the sane and the insane. A question which every saint or moral hero must be capable of *asking* is whether his extraordinary behaviour (perhaps bringing suffering or grief to others) is a product of moral insight or of fanaticism of religious faith or of insantiy. (Note that I insist that the saint or hero must be capable of *asking* this question not *necessarily* of answering it.) The crucial point to be settled now is: what makes such a question possible or intelligible?

As a step towards settling that question we must remind ourselves that the examples we are considering do not belong to the common sense run of ordinary experience. Rich simply could not understand More's point, and in the end there is a relationship between that and More's final demise. Likewise there is a good common sense argument for recommending to Jesus that he accepts the Devil's offer – think of the good he could have achieved in such a position, a mine of argument quarried fully by Dostoevsky's Grand Inquisitor. And, of course, when Jesus did try to forewarn his closest friends of what was to befall him, they, in their good commonsense way, would have none of it. In such a situation the moral hero or saint is driven back on his own resources and into a very radical form of subjectivity indeed. Unfortunately, for the line of argument being pursued, it is in just such radical individuality and subjectivity that we find the ideal breeding ground for fanaticism and, indeed, insanity. Thus it seems that we are making contradictory demands of our moral hero: both that he be willing to accept a radical individuality in his decisions and actions, and also that there be preserved the possibility of drawing a distinction between the individuality of fanaticism and the individuality of heroism.

My contention is that it is precisely at this point that the availability of the language of religion is of fundamental importance. Properly used, the language and thought-forms of religion provide the conceptual space necessary if one is to be able to ask the question 'Could I be wrong?' or 'Might I be deluded?' The saint or moral hero who cannot ask that question is a fanatic or madman in disguise. The language of religion – '. . . and God will know it,' or 'Father, . . . let this cup pass me by . . .' or, 'You shall do homage to the Lord your God and worship him alone' – gives form to the idea of a view *sub specie aeterniatis* which transcends all the limitations and relativities which in cases of extreme individuality are known as madness or fanaticism. In the cases of extreme individualism to which we often apply the description 'moral hero' or 'saint', the possibility of a transcendent order is perhaps the sole means of making intelligible the perspective which the saint must presuppose possible in order to *raise* the question of self-delusion.

The difficulty which faces the saint is this: his goodness is in part defined by its isolation from the norms of his fellows. His resolve depends upon rejecting the norms of others; thus he cannot look to the perspective of those whose values he has rejected in his sainthood in order to be able to fulfil the minimum condition of sanity, i.e. in order to allow, to the extent of finding the question intelligible, that he might just be wrong. Now the perspective of others cannot fill this role, for his sainthood is defined over against the values of the Richs of this world. What is required is a new perspective which stands in relation to his own values, as his own stand to those which he has rejected. Such a perspective is provided by the conception of a transcendent order which expresses the eternal values against which we (even those who are saints) measure our own moral or spiritual insights. Theology articulates the possibility of such a perspective, and in so doing provides the conceptual space essential to the definition of the difference between sainthood and madness or between moral heroism and fanaticism.

To conclude this issue I must summarize and point out one or two further implications of my argument. As More sits in the tower waiting to be executed or as Jesus turns his face towards Jerusalem and execution, what distinguishes them from the fanatical or the insane is the possibility of self-questioning: only the madman excludes *even the possibility* that he might be deluded. Self-questioning requires a perspective other than one's own. Neither Rich nor the disciples could provide that alternative perspective: the argument with them was already over; their values had been found wanting. The only possible perspective which will in the end satisfy the logical demands of the situation is that of a transcendent order of values. Such are the values reflected in 'God will know it' and in the idea of 'thy will'.

However, such values, as eternal, cannot be presented to us as a set of benchmarks against which we measure our own values and those of others. The role of the conception of a view *sub specie aeternitatis* is not descriptive: it is, in Kant's term, 'regulative'. And its regulative role will be quite adequate for our purposes. What More or Jesus require is the idea simply of an order against which their judgements will be assessed. In fact a *list* of 'eternal values' would not do at all, for as soon as formulated and endorsed such a list itself could simply be the expression of fanaticism or insanity. What is at stake in this argument is not the *content* of faith, but, as Kierkegaard stressed, the manner of the appropriation of faith. Faith must be appropriated in a way which distinguishes it from fanaticism. For that it requires the idea of the eternal which transcends even one's most cherished views.

Such an eternal or transcendent order of values understood as the *possibility* of a view *sub specie aeternitatis* is the possibility articulated in theology. We cannot reduce the language of religion in such a way that we no longer articulate this possibility without acknowledging defeat in the whole enterprise of sketching the contours of a life of sainthood or moral heroism. For without the possibility of a perspective in terms of which the saint or hero can *at least ask* 'Might I be deluded?', he is indistinguishable from the fanatic or madman. This is *one* of the reasons for insisting on the importance of More's '. . . and God will know it', *one* of the reasons for the importance of the story of Gethsemane.

In the end, the role of theology, I am arguing, is to articulate the possibility of a perspective *sub specie aeternitatis* on our human affairs. This perspective is regulative in nature and is approached only indirectly through the light which it throws on our world. To lose this perspective, however, is to fail to see our world as it is – it is to have a limited ontology and a defective view of the truth.

8

Jesus, the Eternal and Transcendence

The argument of this book has been that if we are to practise what I have called revisionary theology, we must examine what the constraints and freedoms of a twentieth-century version of Locke's conception of natural religion would be. I have argued that they would be considerable, and that the resultant account of Christianity would be quite unacceptable to some: I respect these reservations, for we deal in matters of great consequence, but I cannot share them. The discussion has been focused primarily on Christianity as a theistic religion, and I hope in the next section of the book to focus upon Christological questions.

I have been elaborating and defending a view of religious belief which does not include belief in God as an individual. This is not unknown outside Christianity, but I cannot pretend that it is in any sense what 'believers have always *really* believed', or that it offers 'the *essence* of *true* Christianity'. Of course not, for the view I am defending is wedded to the notion of the change or development of religious belief. It is not precisely a recommendation about what ought to be believed, it is in fact a concession of what I think *can* be believed. The constraints in question are logical and historical rather than psychological. That they appear as constraints rather than freedoms is also for the moment to be accepted, but they do, I believe, remove unnecessary burdens and, as I hope to show, allow more freedom to respond adequately to problems posed by the historical study of the origins of the

Christian religion, and also to certain pressing contemporary moral and social dilemmas. But these last matters must await a further book.

There are undoubtedly deep dilemmas facing traditional theism in relation to both the moral and the metaphysical attributes of God. The cost of dealing with these adequately to prune belief of any ontological claim that God is (as he is so often believed to be) an individual. It might simply be concluded that the consistent thinker should therefore abandon religious or theistic belief. This, however, would be too quick, and my reasons for this can be summaried by requoting a propositon discussed by Ronald Hepburn, and two sentences from Stuart Hampshire:

> *Hepburn*   If we *were* to abandon all talk of 'God' . . . we should immediately cease to be able to make sense of many things which that concept does make sense of.

> *Hampshire*   . . . the habits and rules of my thinking limit the possibilities of action for me . . .
> The limits of a man's habits of thought are the limits of what he can be expected to try to do . . .

The significance of these remarks, quoted in my first chapter, can now be given clearer expression.

The possibility which has been preserved and expressed in theism, talk of 'God', is the possibility of a view of human affairs '*sub specie aeternitatis*'. Whether this possibility can equally well be preserved in other forms is open to further discussion. I believe that something of the sort is what is to be found in the central books of Plato's *Republic*. Interestingly, the logical problems encountered by Plato are no more easy of solution than those found in theism. The psychological and social power of theism is by comparison a source of profound strength and, therefore, potentially also of profound danger. This must be noted, but requires much more detailed elaboration than can be given to it here.

The possibility of a view *sub specie aeternitatis* is in Hepburn's formulation a means of making 'sense of many things', and in Hampshire's the delineation of 'possibilities of action': that is to say, it is a way of understanding the world and living in it.

How is the believer to understand the world, and to live in it? In one sense this question cannot be answered, for there is no universal recipe for action. We are at best pilgrims who are aware of the possibility of a view *sub specie aeternitatis*, but for whom this is a regulative or formal notion which informs all our thinking without itself being an idea whose content can be separately elaborated. It is the glue which binds together our view of the world rather than being a discriminable item of that view. To affirm that there is such a perspective is, none the less, to enter into ontological commitments: we are claiming that the world tolerates such a possiblity; the structures of reality are thus intelligible.

Christian belief makes claims in this area which distinguish it from other religious and metaphysical beliefs (including alternative versions of theism) and in this chapter I propose to elaborate this point further. In so doing I shall be indicating what it might be to give *Christian* theism the form of natural religion: I shall have the opportunity to integrate more fully into my intellectual tapestry a number of threads of argument left hanging unattached. As you will see, I shall also raise some of the most central problems about the figure of Jesus. These problems are the subject of the next four chapters.

The rest of this chapter will be devoted to a discussion of Bonhoeffer's account of Christian theism. I realize that there is still much controversy about whether the skeletal *Letters and Papers from Prison*[1] were simply a late aberration in his thought. My argument will be that much contained therein was foreshadowed in his lectures on *Christology*.[2] His concern both in 1933 and 1944 was with the problems of transcendence and he was well aware, from his reading of Kant, of all the difficulties of what it means to talk of God. His solution to this problem was never fully worked out, but it contains hints which will allow my central argument to move to its next phase. It will also allow me to give some content to the idea of a life lived *sub specie aeternitatis*.

It is clear that Bonhoeffer is wrestling, in his *Letters and Papers*, not simply with the questions of how to make Christian belief more clear, more 'relevant', or more palatable, to his contemporaries, but rather with substantial questions about the nature and content of Christian belief. One theme in the mosaic of his inquiries which recurs persistently, is that of the doctrine of God. He is particularly preoccupied with the 'beyond' (p. 282) or with what he refers to, variously, as the 'otherness', or the 'transcendence' of God, and even raises, in the notes included under the heading 'Outline for a Book', questions about the sense and reference of the term 'God'.

In *Letters and Papers* as in *Christology*, Bonhoeffer shows himself well aware of the philosophical problems which surround the concept of God. In the former he reviews and rejects the various devices used by believers and theologians to defend the intelligibility of what they say about God. Historically the problem reched definitive form in the writings of Kant: 'since Kant, he [God] has been relegated to a realm beyond the world of experience' (p. 341). Coming, as it does, in the context of some remarks on 'the world . . . come of age', this refers quite clearly to Kant's insistence upon the necessity for ethics, of belief in the autonomy of the human will. The allusion, however, is also to Kant's searing examination of various ways of talking of transcendence, in the *Critique of Pure Reason*. Concepts used 'unschematized', without reference to spatio-temporal co-ordinates, will, Kant argues, generate only confusion or illusion. The consequence of this, that no epistemological route to belief in a transcendent God, or even to the intelligibility of such an idea, is to be found within our empirical experience, had been accepted by many. Several passages, including some of the best known in *Letters and Papers*, are devoted to an attack on those whose evasive tactics indicated that they had not quite grasped the far-reaching significance of Kant's arguments; attacking those, that is to say, who wished to locate God in the gaps of our present knowledge of the universe in which we live, or in the inner life of a man's anxieties and fears. These were, Bonhoeffer believed, the generally accepted contemporary alternatives to various forms of magic and superstition. Each, in their own inadequate way, attempted to give an account of the transcendence of God as a God lying at the limits of human experience and knowledge. Their common fault lay in the picture which each had of the form of an adequate account of the transcendence of God: in contrast to this picture, Bonhoeffer insisted, 'God's "beyond" is not the beyond of our cognitive faculties. The transcendence of epistemological theory has nothing to do with the transcendence of God' (p. 282). Significantly, Bonhoeffer's response to the problem was, if not in detail, at least in general direction, to follow Kant: if theology is to be possible it must be grounded in morality. Whereas for Kant, however, the role of theology was to guarantee a certain sort of consistency and completeness to an already autonomous morality, for Bonhoeffer the relation between theology and morality was one of interdependence.

In order to define the issues more clearly, however, I wish to retrace Bonhoeffer's preoccupation with the concept of transcendence to the 1933 lectures on Christology. In these lectures, at least part of Bonhoeffer's burden is to understand the claim 'God became man'. He rejects as inedquate any metaphysical account of this claim in terms of either essence or *ousia*. Equally unacceptable is any account which would deny the ambiguity of the historical figure. There is no epistemology of faith to be derived from historical study alone: neither through the accounts of a miracle-worker, nor through the portrayal of a sinless or perfect man. 'In christology one looks at the whole historical man Jesus and says of him, "He is God". One does not first look at a human nature and then beyond it to a divine nature; one meets the one man Jesus Christ, who is fully God.' (*Christology*, p. 108) But, of course, men are historical creatures subject to the contingencies of historical existence. The corollaries of this are not to be avoided by regarding the humanity as the husk surrounding the divine kernel to be perceived by the *cognoscenti*. 'Jesus

Christ is the unveiled image of God.' (p. 109) Bonhoeffer is quite uncompromising in his insistence upon 'the weakness . . . the cradle and the cross'. The 'otherness' or 'transcendence' of God is wholly present in this man.

There are two related aspects to this, each central to the theme of the present chapter. On the one hand, there is a view of religious belief, as quite distinct from belief, that rests upon generally accepted epistemological foundations: 'Faith is where the attempt to have security from something visible is rejected' (p. 115). On the other hand, faith, he argues, '. . . is . . . where a man so surrenders himself to the humiliated God-man as to stake his life on him' (pp. 114–15). To anticipate, however, I should want to press the claims of moral insight as a central and constitutive element of that faith. This is not a version of pietism begotten illegitimately in the excesses of romanticism.

The second theme here, which helps provide the link to *Letters and Papers* and to the more general discussion of the concept of transcendence, is Bonhoeffer's refusal to *substitute* the human for the divine, or the immanent for the transcendent, in his theology.

> In humiliation and exaltation, Jesus remains fully man and fully God. The statement 'This is God' must be made of the Humiliated One in just the same way as it is made of the Exalted One.
>
>   We must say of the Humiliated One 'This is God' . . . of this man we say, 'This is God'. Anyone who cannot do this does not know the meaning of 'God became man'. (*Christology*, p. 110)

What is offered here is a set of conditions for understanding the expression 'God became man'. These conditions relate to a particular life and death: '. . . of *this* man we say . . .' This is, of course, very different from the Kantian identification of this man with the supreme example or the archetype of morality, but it does suggest a modification to the believer's concept of God, and his understanding of God's transcendence. As such, it is at once a response to the critique of traditional conceptions of the transcendence of God, and an attempt to move philosophical theology from the shadows cast over it by the *Critique of Pure Reason*.

For Bonhoeffer, the conception of God must be grasped, not merely as 'compatible with', nor simply 'in the light of' the incarnation, but, in fact, only in and through it. This is not to deny the possibility of non-incarnational theologies, nor is it to deny alternative conceptions of God. The essence of his Christology, however, which is Christocentric, is an insistence upon the transformation wrought in the Christian conception of God by the acceptance of the doctrine of the incarnation. If God is to be transcendent, that transcendence has nothing to do with what lies 'beyond' experience, nor with the limitations of scientific knowledge, or with any transcendence defined solely in terms of a particular episte-mological theory. What this leaves is 'the God of Jesus Christ', who, Bonhoeffer tells us, 'has nothing to do with what God, as we imagine him, could do and ought to do. If we are to learn what God promises, and what he fulfils, we must persevere in quiet meditation on the life, sayings, deeds, sufferings, and death of Jesus' (*Letters and Papers*, p. 391). The believer's understanding of God, and of the form of his transcendence, is to be grasped only in the context of meditation upon this man.

The inevitable and legitimate question is, 'Why *this* man?' The question, however, is not simply one of apologetics (although it should arise there also), but is in fact central to the theology in question. The most significant part of Bonhoeffer's skeletal answer, for the purposes of my argu-ment, is his location of the concept of transcendence in the ethical qualities of the 'life, sayings, deeds, sufferings, and death of Jesus'. His 'Outline for a Book' includes the cryptic note: 'His "being there for others" is the experience of trans-cendence. It is only this "being there for others", maintained till death, that is the ground of his omnipotence, omnisci-ence, and omnipresence' (p. 381). The transcendence of God, and reference to the traditional divine transcendent attributes, is firmly located within an ethical conception of the nature of the life and death of Jesus of Nazareth. If we say of 'this man' that he is God, we do so not because of particular miracle-working powers, nor because of the stories surrounding his birth, nor even because of any distinctive, non-ambiguous attributes or capacities. We do so because of the self-giving which may be discerned in his 'weakness'. But such discernment is a *moral* insight: faith is based upon the discernment and affirmation of particular and definitive *ethical* qualities in this man's life and death.

These qualities are not merely the signs indicative of the presence of God. These qualities are definitive of what both the presence of God and the transcendene of God amount to. We have no further conception of transcendence to 'fill out' or 'complete' the ethical. The full note at this point reads:

(b) Who is God? Not in the first place an abstract belief in God, in his omnipotence etc. That is not a genuine experience of God, but a partial extension of the world. Encounter with Jesus Christ. The experience that a transformation of all human life is given by the fact that 'Jesus is there only for others'. His 'being there for others' is the experience of transcendence. It is only this 'being there for others', maintained till death, that is the ground of his omnipotence, omniscience, and omnipresence. Faith is participation in this being of Jesus (incarnation, cross, and resurrection). Our relation to God is not a 'religious' relationship to the highest, most powerful, and best Being imaginable – that is not authentic transcendence – but our relation to God is a new life in 'existence for others', through participation in the being of Jesus. The transcendental is not infinite and unattainable tasks, but the neighbour who is within reach in any given situation. God in human form – not, as in oriental religions, in animal form, monstrous, chaotic, remote, and terrifying, nor in the conceptual forms of the absolute, metaphysical, infinite, etc., nor yet in the Greek divine human form of 'man in himself', but 'the man for others', and therefore the Crucified, the man who lives out of the transcendent. (pp. 381–2)

Clearly Bonhoeffer had a variety of theological targets in his sights in this note, and it is not obviously the case that he intended to make his central point about the transcendence of

God in quite the form in which I am so doing. None the less, the interpretation of the concept of transcendence in ethical terms is compatible with what he wrote, and more significantly for my purposes, a point interesting in its own right is illuminated and clarified by reference to his writings.

The concept of transcendence may be used either absolutely or relatively. If it is used relatively, often hyperbole is involved, as in arguing that one artist transcends all his predecessors. Whether or not that is true, a relative or limited transcendence is of no ultimate interest to the theologian. An absolute transcendence, however, conceived in either metaphysical or epistemological terms, generates the problems of both sense and reference which have preoccupied philosophers and theologians as diverse as Aquinas and Feuerbach, and of which Bonhoeffer was well aware. One alternative is to locate the concept of transcendence within the ethical. This could take the Kantian form of insisting upon the autonomy of morality, and the universality of those moral judgments which are accepted as categorical or absolute. This view, as Iris Murdoch has pointed out,[3] has given an importance to the concepts of 'will' and 'self', which degenerted into what Saul Bellow refers to as 'the Romantic heresy'. Most signficantly, in this form the attempt to understand the concept of transcendence in ethical terms seems to be quite at odds with the Christian conception of 'dying to self'.

A rather different account of absoluteness, or transcendence in ethics can be given, and it is this alternative view which is nearest to the transcendence of which Bonhoeffer speaks. The transcendence involved is the ethical transcendence of the self, not, as in Kantian terms, through the autonomously self-imposed categorical imperative, but through the recognition and acceptance of a demand from without to qualify or give eternal perspective to all that we in our human way might think morally appropriate. It would be a mistake, however, to read too much of Barth, and behind him, Kierkegaard, into these comments. Rather attention should be focused upon two alternative ways of developing these skeletal remarks of Bonhoeffer on the concept of transcendence. In *Letters and Papers*, there has been a shift in emphasis from the centrality given in the lectures on Christology to the weakness and ambiguity of this man Jesus. None the less, the focus in *Letters and Papers* on 'this concern of Jesus for others' extends, rather than supersedes, the earlier work. Both elements are required for the account of transcendence which I wish to offer.

Any account of transcendence in ethical terms will have reference to transcendence of the self, in the sense of the ego. Murdoch writes, 'Moral philosophy is properly, and in the past has sometimes been, the discussion of this ego and of the techniques (if any) for its defeat. In this respect moral philosophy has shared some aims with religion' (*The Sovereignty of Good*, p. 52). Murdoch's essay is an attempt to give an account of what this could amount to for one who is not a religious believer, but who is sensitive to the significance of at least some analogue of the object of religious contemplation, or worship, in any such attempt.

The 'defeat' of the ego, of course, need not involve anything so grand as 'self-transcendence'. The battle between duty and inclination, according to one central tradition within moral thinking, can be fought and won *within* the self. This is not a tradition in which Murdoch is inclined to put a great deal of hope, but it does have the initial advantage of avoiding the problems of giving an account of 'transcendence of the self'. If, however, there is to be a 'defeat' of the ego which is not simply a skirmish within some greater 'self', there must be more than 'technique': there must also be, as Murdoch recognizes, some focus outside 'self'. Traditionally religion has provided this in the concept of God. Both Murdoch and Bonhoeffer are aware of the conceptual problems surrounding this idea. Whereas, however, Murdoch looks towards some analogue of the Platonic form of the good to provide such a focus for contemplation, Bonhoeffer, as we have seen, gives focus to his contemplation by insisting, 'we must persevere in quiet meditation on the life, sayings, deeds, sufferings and death of Jesus.' The absolute importance of an external, and in that sense objective, point to which we may direct our gaze, cannot be underestimated if our business is to escape from the demands of self. Neither Bonhoeffer, nor Murdoch, however, is concerned with a *metaphysical* absorption of self into what is not self, but with an *ethical* liberation from the demands of the self.

Thus, the grounds for turning to Jesus' life and death as the focus of our meditation are ethical. It is not simply, however, a matter of finding the perfect example of our already formed moral beliefs, although the initial attraction is at least partially to our moral sensitivities. For in addition to being the focus which directs us away from self in our thinking and feeling, he does define for us the nature of that other form of self-transcendence, viz. concern for others. Two quotations from Murdoch may help make plain the sense of this:

> Freedom is not strictly the exercise of will, but rather the experience of accurate vision which, when this becomes appropriate, occasions action. (p. 67)

> The more the separateness and differentness of other people is realized, and the fact seen that another man has needs and wishes as demanding as one's own, the harder it becomes to treat a person as a thing. (p. 66)

Transcendence of the ego, or the self, can be spoken of in terms of a type of freedom, but it cannot be the freedom of one part of the self to subdue another. The freedom *from* self in this sense is the accuracy of vision which one has of another being or person, which becomes absorbed in the needs and distinctiveness of that other person. This absorption is referred to by Simone Weil as the quality of 'loving attention'. It is an extension of the remarks we have already noted from Bonhoeffer's *Letters and Papers*.

> The experience that a transformation of all human life is given by the fact that 'Jesus is there only for others'. His 'being there for others' is the experience of transcendence. . . . The transcendental is not infinite and unattainable tasks, but the neighbour who is within reach in any given situation. (p. 381)

Thus, for Bonhoeffer, Jesus of Nazareth is both the object of meditation – which Murdoch sees as an essential aspect in the atempt to 'defeat' the ego, and to transcend self – and also the image of that transcendence which is concern for, or loving attention to, others. On either count, however, the transcendence at issue is ethical.

A different but complementary perspective may be gained on the search for transcendence by turning to the feature of the life of Jesus stressed by Bonhoeffer in *Christology*. There he places considerable emphasis upon the weakness and the ambiguity in that life and death. The ambiguity, of course, resides in part in the weakness, because *prima facie* it is not obvious that the crucifixion was an expression of omnipotence. There is, Bonhoeffer argues, 'no such thing as this divine essence. If Jesus Christ is to be described as God, then we may not speak of this divine essence, of his omnipotence and his omniscience, but we must speak of this weak man among sinners, of his cradle and his cross' (p. 108). In Bonhoeffer's theology, the weakness of this man is offered as an account of wherein his divinity resides. This is, of course, a transformation of the notion of divinity. Transcendence is now envisaged, not after the model of Imperial Rome, but after the model of one of its victims. It is, in part at least, of self-abnegation which Bonhoeffer speaks, but neither is it simply the self-denial of conquered desires, nor, as his comments on the limitations of Kenoticism make plain, is it the self-emptying of God.

There is a further ethical dimension here to the weakness of the cradle and the cross. If a man's ethical intent is some form of integrity or selflessness, then this very intent can be the most insidious temptation of all. Selflessness of this sort can become the fanatical search for a purity which separates one from one's fellow human beings, both in so far as it can secretly feed the furnaces of a white-hot pride, and also in so far as it creates a fear of contamination. This man, however, is selfless, not so much in what he does as in what he suffers. Such, however, might be thought to preclude the very possibility of talk of transcendence. To argue in this way is to

confine the concept of transcendence in an unwarranted
fashion.

To speak of transcendence is to speak of what is not subject
to limits or constraints. To speak of ethical transcendence is
to attempt to overcome in one's ethical existence those external and internal pressures which threaten to modify or relati-
vize our ethical outlook. The external pressures in question
largely derive from our nature as social creatures. The tension between the ideals of withdrawal and involvement
which we find in religions as diverse as Christianity and
Buddhism signpost clearly the issues at stake.

The natural instinct of those who refuse to seek integrity
through withdrawal is to protect themselves, at least from
those who would seek radically to harm or hinder the process
of ethical growth. The teaching implicit in 'the life, sayings,
deeds, sufferings, and death of Jesus' is that it is only if
evasive action is ruled out from the start (the weakness of the
cradle), and if the vulnerability to what men may do to one is
total (the weakness of the cross), that one is in the ethical
sense 'invulnerable'. This is not to imply any necessity in
this: there is no guaranteed technique here. But what is
offered is an account of the conditions of the possibility of
ethical transcendence: whatever they did to him, men were
unable to corrupt him. Only in his total self-abandonment to
the will of others is it made clear that ethically he cannot be
harmed.

This, of course, is a lesson which Socrates taught, and
aspects of which have been explored with varying degrees of
success and insight in the novels of Dostoevsky, Jaroslav
Hasek, and Joseph Heller. One major distinction between
Jesus and Socrates lies in the emphasis upon weakness in the
case of Jesus: an emphasis possible only because of the transformation of the theological concept of divine transcendence
which is taking place. A further substantial diference lies in
the emphasis in Bonhoeffer's account of Jesus, on Jesus as
'the man for others'. At both of these points there is resist-
ance to any suggestion of an ethical identification of Jesus and
Socrates.

The central point, however, has been to clarify the sense in which the notion of transcendence with which Bonhoeffer is working, is ethical. The case for this lies in the primacy of recognizing this man as God or as divine, in virtue of, and *solely* in virtue of 'his life, sayings, deeds, sufferings and death'.

A note of summary and transition to the third and final section of the book is necessary. Drawing upon writers as varied in their commitments as Dietrich Bonhoeffer and Iris Murdoch, I have been trying to establish the intelligibility of a notion of transcendence which is essentially ethical in character. The transcendence of Jesus, in this view, is to be understood as a recognition of his divinity which *is* a view of 'his life, sayings, deeds, sufferings and death'. It is the view of these, in which they exemplify and thus declare the intelligibility of the idea of a perspective on this world which sees the world as one, which is *sub specie aeternitatis*.

Two questions must be asked of such a claim, of which the first is the more difficult. Why *this* man? And can a historical individual bear the weight thus being placed upon the contingencies of his life? Rather circuitous answers will be offered to these questions in the last section of the book. Pro tem it will be useful to note that this allows me to move from a general account of theism as 'the definition, protection and expression of the possibility of a view of the world *sub specie aeternitatis*', to a more specific exploration of Christian theism as an examination of the contribution of the figure of Jesus to the definition of such a possibility.[4]

Part III

The Ambiguous Figure of Jesus

9

History and Faith

In the next four chapters I intend to examine the figure of Jesus and the extent to which the general approach which I have defined in relation to the concept of God, allows an adequate response to him. Of course, what counts as 'adequate' in this context will be a matter of some dispute. What will not be disputed is that an inevitable first step in any discussion of these questions must be a survey of some of the issues arising under the heading of 'History and Faith'. Immediately, however, I step onto thin ice, and that for two reasons: firstly, the area is much-disputed territory, and secondly, some of the arguments are properly the province of those more skilled than I in historical, textual, and linguistic studies. None the less, even the most outspoken champions of Biblical criticism would admit that there are some questions here which reasonably require philosophical comment, and my own inclination is to regard these philosophical issues as of fundamental importance.

Although I cannot assent to the simplification that regards the idea of history as a modern invention – surely Thucydides was no mere uncritical chronicler – none the less the theological and philosophical problems of the relationship between history and faith do for a variety of reasons have a distinctively recent form to them. The formidable nature of these difficulties, however, has not come fresh from the mould; rather it has grown by accretion, as if over several generations care was not taken to fully scour the mould of theological reflection before it was put to new use. Thus a residue has built up, which gives a shape less than elegant, with rather unclear structure, to what is surely one of the dominating intellectual concerns of contemporary theology – the extent to which the growth in the centrality given to an awareness of history in European thought will alter our appreciation of the character of faith.

Thus it is arguable that the implications of Erasmus' transposition of the principles of textual criticism normally applied to non-scriptural classical texts, to the production of a Greek edition of the New Testament in 1516, has still to be fully absorbed into theological discussion. There is much more to this than a protest against rearguard actions by literalist versions of biblical fundamentalism: what is at stake is the perception of the religious texts of Christianity as documents with a history, and indeed of Christianity itself *from at least one point of view*, as a historical phenomenon – with all that that entails about questions which may be appropriately asked of and put to it. The very process of editing religious texts in this way raises in absolutely crucial form the central questions about the relation of God to his creation, and the manner of his self-manifestation or self-revelation. If, as in traditional forms of belief, he has manifested or revealed himself in Jesus, or in the gospels which bear witness to him, then that form of belief cannot any longer refuse to reckon with the fact that this man or these books are themselves part of a shifting changing network of things, people, times and places which are bound to us and we to them by varying degrees of epistemological approximation.

There were, of course, many steps on the way, many layers of accretion, whether through the hidden scholarship of Reimarus, or the sophisticated duplicities of Lessing which helped bring Reimarus' work to posthumous light – or whether through the influence of Hegel, brought to bear on the world of biblical criticism by F. C. Baur and quite seminally by D. F. Strauss's *Life of Jesus* (1835–6). Van A. Harvey describes well how Troeltsch gave definitive form to one

major consequence of this in his insistence that historical
enquiry was essentially critical in character and that as such
its results were inevitably incompatible with orthodox
Christian belief:

> [Troeltsch] argued that critical historical inquiry rests on three
> interrelated principles: (1) the principle of criticism, by which
> he meant that our judgements about the past cannot simply be
> classed as true or false but must be seen as claiming only a
> greater or lesser degree of probability and as always open to
> revision; (2) the principle of analogy, by which he meant that
> we are able to make such judgements of probability only if we
> presuppose that our own present experience is not radically
> dissimilar to the experience of past persons; and (3) the princi-
> ple of correlation, by which he meant that the phenomena of
> man's historical life are so related and interdependent that no
> radical change can take place at any one point in the historical
> nexus without effecting a change in all that immediately
> surrounds it. Historical explanation therefore necessarily
> takes the form of understanding an event in terms of its
> antecedents and consequences, and no event can be isolated
> from its historically conditioned time and space.[1]

In a different context James Barr refers to the difficulty as an
antinomy, 'between history as the milieu of God's confessed
action and history as a milieu subject to human critical
examination'.[2] Barr's target on that occasion was those who
would attempt to avoid or resolve the antinomy by the
twofold strategy of reinterpreting the categories of history
and revelation and either explicitly or implicitly suggesting
that these reinterpreted notions were to be found – at least by
the discerning eye – in the Bible. I have neither the wit nor
the inclination to contest Barr's judgment: 'Ultimately "history", when used as an organizing and classifying bracket, is
not a biblical category' (p. 69). Indeed I would push the point
further and suggest that certain strands of theology have
created for themselves an insoluble problem by looking to
the biblical texts for a solution to a post-biblical problem
about the relationship between God and the historical order,
which is in fact also a problem about the nature of the Bible

to which the biblical authors did not address themselves. The advantage of Barr's (earlier) formulation over Harvey's is that it makes absolutely clear that the problems of the relation of history and faith are neither purely biblocentric nor Christocentrics, they are essentially theocentric for they challenge the very basis of the traditional account of the relation between God and the world.

Manifestly, the problems of the relationship between history and faith are complex: equally certain is the fact that their origin is to be found not in the intellectual snares of Satan, nor in the malevolence of those whose aim is to destroy faith. Many of the major problems have arisen from the legitimate intertwining of the aims of both piety and scholarship, viz. the better understanding of the Christian Scriptures. However,

> The fact – the plain inescapable fact which has to be accepted – is that there is wide diversity of interpretation; and where scholars of undoubted competence and integrity diverge so widely, no reconstruction of events can lay exclusive claim to be regarded as historical in the normal modern sense of the word.[3]

Of course, there have always been disagreements about the interpretation of the Scriptures, but the rise of the application of historical, linguistic and textual critical methods to the sacred writings of the dominant religion of the culture poses particular problems: for our culture is formed both by the religion of Christianity *and* by the systematic extension of critical thought into the very foundations of the picture which we have of ourselves, our society, and the world in which we live. The outcome, however, has not been unanimity. Maurice Wiles catches one element of the resultant mood well when he writes, 'The rise of modern historical consciousness has, in some degree or another, made historical relativists of us all.'[4] The qualification in that remark is, however, important. A divergence of views amongst experts does not inevitably lead to relativism, but it does constitute a particular problem when the disagreements in question are over the fundamentals of faith. The problem becomes that of the relationship of 'believer' to 'expert', and this is a problem which the ecclesiastical establishment has often handled very badly.

At the heart of the difficulties lies the question of the figure of Jesus, and there have been three major proposals for providing a theological account of the role of Jesus. I shall sketch these in general terms, illustrating the three as general tendencies which are each capable of a variety of emphases.

In the first place, there are those who see the main danger as endemic uncertainty. With great perception Kierkegaard warns us of the consequences of giving place to historical enquiry: '. . . nothing is more readily evident than that the greatest attainable certainty with respect to anything historical is merely an *approximation*. And an approximation, when viewed as a basis for an eternal happiness, is wholly inadequate, since the incommensurability makes a result impossible.'[5] The more recent debates on this theme have focused on the question of whether historical research can provide support for or, perhaps more worryingly, falsify the claims of faith. A number of contemporary theologians have confronted this point by trying to separate the claims of history from those of faith. Paul Tillich, for example, writes, 'Historical research can neither give nor take away the foundations of the Christian faith.'[6] His statement implies that the truth or falsehood of the historical beliefs is of no relevance to the truth or falsehood of Christian faith. To the following extent I should agree with him: historical research cannot *give* the foundations of the Christian faith. Nothing that the research historian can do could *prove* or verify Christian faith. No amount of historical knowledge about the life of Jesus of Nazareth will guarantee or verify that he is the Christ, the Son of God. History does not *prove* faith and in that sense cannot compel it. In one sense, to be elaborated later, when one knows all that there is to know about this man, he is still an ambiguous figure. As Bonhoeffer argued in his lectures on Christology, no further piece of historical information can remove this ambiguity.

A further insight which is shared by Tillich and others is the realization that historicity implies risk: if one does insist upon the historicity of some of the central claims of the Christian faith, then one puts that faith at risk. It *could* in principle be shown to be substantially misguided. It is just such a fear which Paul Van Buren expresses when he writes, '. . . the Christian [might] be at the mercy of the historian, so that if historical judgement were to repaint the picture of Jesus, the character or content of faith would have to shift with the historical reconstruction.'[7] I should want to insist that the price for making particular historical beliefs central or essential to one's faith is the risk of falsification. One's faith is then historically vulnerable.

The risk of vulnerability is a high price to pay, and many theologians, including Tillich and Van Buren, have refused to pay it. The only legitimate refusal must be based on a complete rejection of the importance of historical facts. Such an extreme conclusion is adopted by Harvey in *The Historian and the Believer*. He argues, 'The conclusion one is driven to is that the content of faith can as well be mediated through a historically false story *of a certain kind* as through a true one, through a myth as well as through history' (pp. 280–1). Harvey's conclusion is well argued, and if one refuses to adopt it one has to face a particularly awkward question: what is it about Christian faith that demands the truth of particular historical beliefs? What *would* be lost that is essential to Christian faith if some of these historical beliefs were found to be false? I shall return to this question when I have sketched out the two further main theological responses to the problem of the relation of history to faith.

The second position is the attempt to use historical methods to derive from biblical (and where relevant non-biblical) material an account of the historical Jesus. The nineteenth century produced its crop of lives of the historical Jesus. Each of them was of course a sifting and restructuring of the biblical evidence, and each of them was different. In fact it was at this time that the full impact of scholarly disagreement began to be felt in the minds of the believers and in the councils of the churches. But if this approach can be sustained so it is claimed, the problem of the relationship of faith to history can be solved. There is some truth in this, but only a half-truth.

If the major difficulty in the way of linking faith and history is historical scepticism, then surely it is true that if the claims of faith are justified, good historical scholarship will not in the end be at odds with the content of that faith. In general, for example,

> Practically no serious scholar doubts that in the first half-century of our era a figure called Joshua – or in Greek, Jesus – travelled round in Palestine carrying out an activity of exorcizing and of counselling, teaching and preaching, often in parables, that he fell foul of the Jewish authorities and was eventually crucified by the Romans.[8]

The hopes of the traditional quest for the historical Jesus rested on the possibility of extending that consciousness to the construction of a recognizable picture of the external form of Jesus' life. There were in due course even bolder spirits who proposed that we might be able to give some account of Jesus' view of himself and his work. The essential point, however, is that this approach focuses on what historical enquiry can tell us about Jesus in the hope and trust that it will in the end be seen to be supportive rather than destructive of faith.

None the less, as I have suggested, this deals with only half of the problem. If the difficulty is restricted to the problems which historical scepticism can pose to faith, then this is undoubtedly the only way to deal with it. But the qualifying phrase, that 'in the end' it is the hope of the believer that the concent of belief about, say, the figure of Jesus will be at one with the results of historical enquiry, still leaves quite untouched the point made by Kierkegaard: can and need the eternal significance of faith wait on the results of historical enquiry which can at best be approximate and revisable in principle? Kierkegaard draws the most important related distinction between the results of what we might call 'pure' scholarship, and those of a rather different sort of 'scholarship' which promises, albeit implicitly, a result for faith – between 'philological scholarship' and 'the scholarly critical theology', whose 'entire procedure suffers from a certain conscious or unconscious ambiguity. It constantly seems as if this labour of criticism were suddenly about to yield a result for faith, issuing in something relevant to faith. Here lies the difficulty' (op. cit. p. 27). The philologist, the historian and the textual critic can produce the best possible text (as Erasmus did), or the best possible historical reconstruction as Strauss and the others attempted to do, but '. . . when he has finished, nothing follows except the wholly admirable result that an ancient writing has now through his skill and competence received its most accurate possible form. But by no means that I should now base my eternal happiness on this work . . .' (ibid.) As Kierkegaard makes plain, his intention is not to disparage the work of the specialist here; but he is insisting that there is a logical gap between historical scholarship and faith. The reason is that the results of even the best scholarship are in principle revisable – a point well-elaborated by Harvey.

The same difficulties will arise for those writers who have more recently rallied under the banner of the 'new quest' for the historical Jesus. This movement has a variety of manifestations, but while its adherents have considerable respect for the questions of the historical scepticism which swept away the 'old quest' for the historical Jesus, they have not succumbed to the attractions of the radical disjunction of history and faith which we have seen exemplified in Kierkegaard, Tillich, and Harvey. Ernst Fuchs, for example, grants much of what lies behind such an approach, and of a corresponding tendency amongst New Testament critics to diminish the significance of the *prima facie* narrative/historical style of the Synoptics:

> But granting all of that, will one not have to ask all the more: How does it happen that the Gospels want to narrate words and deeds of the historical Jesus, as Matthew, Mark and Luke have clearly done? To be sure, what is at issue is not how

many of these words are 'authentic' and which acts of Jesus actually happened. Rather, what is decisive is the fact that such things should be narrated at all. What does this interest of the evangelists mean?[9]

Fuchs asks absolutely the right question, and offers his own answer – in Jesus, no less than in the apostles, God's word is to be heard. In passing, it must be said that the very fact that a distinguished New Testament critic in the mid-twentieth century has to put the point in this way is a point worthy of the irony of Kierkegaard: 'So one illuminates the other. Jesus illuminates the apostles' talk and their talk illuminates Jesus' task. *This is why I have in my own way renewed the question of the historical Jesus*' (ibid. p. 136). My admiration for Fuchs, however, relates to his identification of an important question, rather than in his weak answer. The inadequacy of the answer is that it does not reckon with either Kierkegaard's point, nor with the very deep-seated scepticism and widespread disagreement about almost all of the doctrinally central elements of Jesus' life and sayings. Professor Nineham, quoted earlier, has no such illusions. He points clearly to the whole range of theologically crucial matters about which there is no consensus at all – for example Jesus' claims about himself, his views about his own death, the possibility of resurrection and what happened in the three or four days after his crucifixion. None the less, Fuchs's question about the interest of the gospel-writers in the historical Jesus is a fair one and I shall return to it in due course.

So far I have outlined two different responses to the problem of the relation of history to faith – the radical separation of faith from historical belief and enquiry (Kierkegaard, Tillich, *et al.*), and the various forms of the so-called 'new quest' for the historical Jesus. I must now outline briefly the third main type of response – as radical as it is provocative. There is to hand in Schubert Ogden's 1980 Sarum Lectures a concise restatement of this third position, and we can treat this as a representative example.

Ogden is quite unimpressed by the 'new quest' as an adequate response to the complex problems which we are facing. His main concern is that the new quest differs from the old quest only in detail and not in essential structure. The new quest he regards as 'revisionary' rather than (presumably) as 'revolutionary':

> One of the common characteristics of revisionary movements generally is that they tend to exhibit more extensive agreement with the traditional positions to which they are revisions than persons on either side are likely to realize. Thus even if they do not agree in giving the same answer, they nevertheless do agree in asking the same question.[10]

Ogden correctly points out that common to all forms of preoccupation with the historical figure of Jesus – whether 'new' or 'old' – is the centrality of the question, 'Who is Jesus?' He is prepared to tolerate one understanding of this question, *viz*. when it is a question 'about the meaning of Jesus for us', but he suspects the consensus which treats the question in its prima facie sense, as a question 'about the being of Jesus himself'.

There are two further points of agreement between the revisionary and traditional forms of Christological discussion and stating these will help clarify the radical nature of Ogden's alternative proposals. The first is that new and old preoccupations with the figure of Jesus agree in identifying the Christ of faith with the Jesus of history, '. . . in so far as he can be known to us today by way of empirical–historical inquiry using the writings of the New Testament as sources' (pp. 16–17). The further point of consensus is a belief that whatever must be true of a subject for that subject to be the Christ, must be true of 'the particular subject', Jesus.

Now Ogden offers criticisms of each of these assumptions, but in the end there are two main points which he wishes to stress: the first, already mentioned, is that these assumptions show that the gap between 'traditional' and 'revisionary' accounts of Christology are too close for revisionary comfort. The second main point is best seen in the elaboration of his own alternative account, which, to be concise, argues that the central question of Christology should be an 'existential–

historical' one which 'asks about the meaning of Jesus for us here and now in the present, not about the being of Jesus in himself then and there in the past' (p. 41). Things, however, are not quite as simple as the selection of this particular quotation might imply, for Ogden is not prepared to reject totally the questions of historical enquiry.

In fact, the reverse is affirmed, for it is claimed (p. 62) that empirical–historical enquiry is 'very definitely a theological necessity'. The reason for this prima facie discrepancy is that Ogden's position is the product of a series of tensions which will in the end result in a breaking-point. That point is reached in the consideration of the place of historical enquiry. There are two points in Ogden's position which require careful scrutiny: the first is his insistence upon the primacy of the earliest witnesses; the second is his distinction between what the witnesses assert and what they assume.

He is absolutely firm on the first of these points, and there seem to be three aspects to it. The earliest witnesses are primary for faith in that they are the focus of historical and theological enquiry. To be blunt, it is 'their' Jesus which is 'the real subject of the Christological assertion' (p. 63), rather than the historical figure who lived in Palestine. A consequence of this about which he is clear is that the 'theologically necessary' task of empirical–historical enquiry is to analyse the New Testament writings in search of the earliest possible 'stratum of the traditional witness lying behind them'. A second consequential issue about which he is less precise, for he does not think the issue is important, is whether what the earliest witnesses affirm about Jesus is to be regarded as in any sense normative for what is true about the historical figure. He ought to address this point rather more clearly than he does. What is quite certain, according to Ogden, is that the earliest witness to Jesus is not the basis for either historical or Christological construction, but is 'itself the norm of appropriateness'. One cannot but infer from the context that the appropriateness in question refers to 'existential–historical' rather than 'empirical–historical' claims. There are several serious difficulties about this view, and I shall enumerate three of them. All three will exemplify my main concern that he has not adequately clarified the relationship between history and faith, or, in his terms, between 'existential–historical' and 'empirical–historical' affirmations.

Ogden's objections to the revisionary type of Christology are both historical and theological in character. On the one hand he is sceptical about the possibility of establishing of the historical Jesus, as distinct from the Jesus experienced and remembered, that he did or said any particular deed or word attributed to him. On the other hand, even if it was possible, 'there would still be the decisive objection that the Jesus attested by the Christian witness is infinitely other and more than the so-called historical Jesus' (p. 112). The point here is that if there is such an infinite gap between the Jesus of faith and the Jesus of history then we run the risk of adopting a view which is compatible with the claim that the Jesus of faith is a construct, possibly an invention of those who came after him and testify to him. I have already conceded that historical enquiry cannot prove or verify the claims of faith, but it does seem as if formally Ogden is adopting the position where the claims of faith are compatible with any and every historical claim about Jesus of Nazareth.

It does at one point appear that Ogden relents and allows an important role to historical enquiry, perhaps comparable to the position adopted by Fuchs. He does in fact discuss the 'Christology' of Jesus, and thus, it seems, gives some positive role to the historical questions which may be set in this area. However, any apparent move to allow significance to these historical questions is quickly reversed in a passage which is as clear on this point as it is ambiguous on their implications. Ogden allows that at best there may be room for talk of 'Jesus' *implied* Christology' (my italics). He then stresses that there was no explicit Christology in the way in which Jesus thought and spoke of himself, and continues,

> But in making the judgement that this is indeed a reasonable empirical–historical account, I am quite certain that it is in no way necessary to a constructive Christology of reflection such

as I am seeking to develop in this book. Whether Jesus did or did not make the kind of claim of which the church's Christ-ological assertion is the explication in no way alters the fact that, even in the earliest stratum of witnesses accessible to us, what is meant by Jesus – and the *only* thing that is meant by him – is the one who makes or at any rate implies such a claim. (pp. 120–1)

The main point which I wish to make is that if we are talking of a Christology which is 'implicit' in Jesus, then we are not restricted to what Jesus implied by his words: we are inevit-ably and rightly raising the question of which affirmations about Jesus are compatible with the man who was Jesus. No matter how sceptical we may be about answers to this ques-tion, the sense and importance of the question cannot be properly denied.

The ambiguities in Ogden's position are associated with his use of the word 'meant'. There is a confusion between one use in which some may care to say something like 'Jesus meant a great deal to me' and a more formal use in which one uses the word 'Jesus' as a definite description, rather than a name, and in which the definite description is given the meaning 'the one who makes or at any rate implies such a claim'. The word 'Jesus' so used (normally in conjunction with the word 'Christ') is then easily detached from the historical figure of Jesus for it has a perfectly good meaning which does not depend on there being a historical individual to which it is attached as a proper name: 'what Jesus means to me' is transformed without remainder into 'what "Jesus" means', i.e. 'the one who makes or at any rate implies such a claim' – of 'decisive significance'.

The third difficulty which I find with Ogden's Christology is that despite his insistence that 'the christology of reflection, being fully critical, asks about the truth of the christology of witness as well as about its meaning' (pp. 3–4), he is in the end epistemologically naïve. The question which he simply ignores as if it did not arise is: Which witnesses to the signifi-cance of Jesus are witnesses to the truth about Jesus? Do we listen to those who called him a blasphemer and breaker of the law? Or to those who preferred the release of Barabas? Or to the followers of Muhammad who give him a place of significance, albeit not a decisive one? The move which substitutes historical enquiry into the earliest tradition about Jesus for historical enquiry into Jesus, may ease the problems of historical enquiry, but it does nothing to ease the important epistemological question of why we should pay any attention to this tradition if our interest is in the end the truth of the matter. The fact that a particular tradition happens to have survived, and for perhaps good authoritarian or ecclesiastical reasons happens to be glorified by the name 'apostolic witness', carried no epistemological weight. And of course the difficulty is compounded if it seems that whatever this tradition says about Jesus is deemed to be true because 'Jesus' is no longer a proper name, but is the description whose content is settled by appeal to what these witnesses say.

The problems which are thus left unresolved in Ogden's thought are to be set alongside the difficulties encountered in the two other approaches to the matter of the relationship between history and faith outlined earlier in this chapter, *viz.* the Tillichian rejection of any significance of history for faith, and the quest for the historical Jesus, whether of the old or new variety. The Tillichian approach prompted the question: What would be lost that is essential to Christian faith if some of these historical beliefs (about Jesus) were found to be false? And from the approach of 'New quester', Ernst Fuchs, we noted and retained for further discussion the questions: 'How does it happen that the Gospels want to narrate words and deeds of the historical Jesus? . . . what is decisive is the fact that such things should be narrated at all. What does this interest of the evangelists mean?' Ogden ignores these questions, though on his approach surely at least the second is unavoidable. I propose now to attempt to answer them, and to begin by sketching two very different examples of the relationship between history and beliefs.

In Rome in 1617, during the building of St Peter's, some relics were found which were believed to be fragments of the

True Cross. In honour of the occasion Monteverdi wrote and arranged the first performance of a particularly beautiful five-part motet. It is doubtful whether anyone now alive believes that these relics were fragments of the True Cross; it is even doubtful whether these relics still exist. Monteverdi's motet, however, has been preserved and is still performed regularly. The historical belief which was the occasion of its composition is now discredited, yet the music is no less delightful, nor at all diminished in quality or value.

Sometimes, what we value especially highly is connected in one way or another with particular historical beliefs. Sometimes the connection is such that we may come to see these historical beliefs as mistaken without changing our valuation or regard for whatever it is that we connect with the beliefs. In such cases we may say that the historical belief is *externally related* to the attitude, evaluation, or belief that tends to accompany it: that is, the historical belief may be severed or cast off without substantial loss to its erstwhile companion. The case which I have just quoted is an example of the sort of relationship which I have in mind.

Let us consider a different sort of example. In a foreword to his book *Culloden*, John Prebble writes: 'The book begins with Culloden because then began a sickness from which Scotland, and the Highlands in particular, never recovered. It is a sickness of the emotions and its symptoms can be seen on the labels of whisky bottles.' The sickness, or attitude, or set of attitudes, of which Prebble speaks, shows itself in sentimental and highly coloured views of Scotland, and particularly of those parts of it which lie to the west and north of a line drawn from Glasgow, through Stirling and Perth to Aberdeen. One of its roots is certainly Sir Walter Scott's imaginative and gifted story-telling. Its result is a *kind* of patriotism on the part of some Scotsmen and a romanticizing on the part of transatlantic descendants of Scottish emigrants. Part of these attitudes is a set of historical beliefs which are by and large false: for example that all the clans, except the traitor Campbells, rose as soon as Prince Charles raised his standard; that men went willingly, even eagerly, to support the Jacobite cause; and that Culloden was a last gallant and glorious stand against the ruthless overpowering odds of the Duke of Cumberland's war-machine. That the Duke of Cumberland could be ruthless is more than probable; otherwise the rest is a tissue of fantasy, as Prebble's book clearly demonstrates.

To see the fantasy for what it is, to see the historical beliefs as quite unfounded, is, if not to destroy, at least radically to alter the sentimental romanticizing: in Prebble's terms, it is to diagnose the sickness as a sickness, and to lay the basis for its cure. In this instance the historical beliefs are *internally* related to the complex of attitudes, beliefs and evaluations in question. To see these historical beliefs as false is to alter substantially one's relationship to, say, one's native land.

In producing these two different examples I am trying to define the question which I want finally to consider in this chapter: the question of the relationship between particular historical beliefs and Christian faith. To use the terms in which I have characterized, respectively, my two examples, are the historical beliefs *externally* or *internally* related to the religious faith? Can the historical beliefs be shown false, and their relationship to the religious faith be severed, without substantial loss or alteration to that faith? Or is the faith somehow bound up with the beliefs so that their falsification is faith's embarrassment?

The fact that the historical beliefs which stimulated Monteverdi are in fact false leaves the motet which he composed quite untouched. In the other case, however, the particular brand of sentimental patriotism or romanticizing to which Prebble takes exception has, as a constitutive element, particular historical beliefs which are false. The question which faces us is: Are the beliefs which are historically vulnerable in any way constitutive of Christian faith? If so, in what way?

It might be argued that they are not. That what is constitutive if faith is something else – say a particular set of moral teachings, those attributed to Jesus. Now if what is constitutive of faith is the acceptance of the moral teachings of Christ, then it does not matter if these are *his* teachings or anyone else's. They stand on their own feet. If they do command one's moral allegiance, they do so for what they are in themselves, irrespective of who first uttered them. The historical beliefs are non-essential, non–constitutive of faith.

Or again, it might be argued that the account which we have of the life of Jesus reveals what is fundamental about the life of men: it tells man of the nature of the transcendent God, and of his relationship to that God. It provides men with the possibility of knowledge.

These two possibilities respectively present Jesus as the Teacher and the Revealer. (Interestingly enough, these are the two roles upon which Harvey's discussion of Christ particularly fastens.) If this is the relationship of the believer to Christ, that of the pupil to the teacher, that of the one to whom truths are revealed to the revealer, then, as Kierkegaard insists in *Philosophical Fragments*, in one sense it does not matter who the teacher is, who the revealer is. The teacher may be a historical figure, Jesus of Nazareth, or the teacher may in fact be the writer who created a mythical figure, whom he called Jesus of Nazareth, to act as his mouthpiece – in the same sort of way as Sir Roger de Coverley acts as the mouthpiece of Joseph Addison. The fact that Sir Roger never lived, or that the person upon whom he is modelled differs from him in certain important respects, matters not at all: Addison's comment upon the ways of men is as pungent as ever.

Or again, if Jesus of Nazareth is regarded as giving us, in his life, a supreme example of self-giving which ought to inspire imitation, then in one sense it matters not at all whether this is history or fiction. The point is that the story defines the possibility of such a way of life. Whether or not the life was historically lived as the story depicts it does not matter. We now know that such a way of life is a possibility, and that is what is really important in an example: it shows a possibility. A novel could do so equally well.

What is becoming clear is that the question of the role of particular historical beliefs in Christian faith cannot be considered in isolation. Already the central problem of Christology has been raised: Who is Jesus of Nazareth? What do we make of this man? The two issues are related in this way: if the relationship between particular historical beliefs and Christian faith is *external*, then our Christology must take the form of seeing the divinity of Christ in his role as teacher, revealer and example. Conversely, if seeing Jesus as divine is completely expressed in terms of seeing him in these three roles, teacher, revealer and example, then we need not feel a final commitment to any particular historical beliefs.

On the other hand, if we do want to insist upon particular historical beliefs as internally related to, or (partly) constitutive of, Christian faith, then amongst other things this must commit us to a different account of the divinity of Christ. I shall return to this as I go on to try to show what it means to say that the historical beliefs are internally related to Christian faith.

The crucial question still remains: What difference does a set of historical beliefs make to Christian faith?

Initially it allows for a particular kind of development or growth of insight on the part of the believer. The notion of insight is important here. The growth or development is in part at least a result of what we *find* in this life and death: it is not simply a matter of what we fashion or create for ourselves. That there was a particular historical existence is important in two ways and .for two different groups of people. In the first instance it is important in that it gives sense to the possibility of setting limits to what faith can be, to what can be said about Christ and about God. If his life was of this form or that, then not anything can be said of Jesus of Nazareth; some things are ruled out from the start. That he died as he did, for example, at least rules out the account of him as a successful revolutionary military commander. In the second instance, if the focus and origin of faith is a particular historical life, if faith is, in part at least, seeing the significance of that life, then the idea that we can give a once-and-for-all account of what it is to believe will be ruled out. A historical life is a group of contingent events. The significance of contingent events cannot be summarized finally and definitively, the facts can always be regrouped and seen in the light of new experience.

The two groups of people to whom this makes a difference are the writers of the New Testament, particularly of the Gospels, and contemporary believers. In the case of the former group it means that one can look for and expect to find growth and development of insight, even within the New Testament. If it is to be growth of insight rather than difference in the powers of imagination, then the historical content of Christian faith must be retained as crucial. Closely related to this is the logically prior need to make *intelligible* the claim that the Gospel writers have presented us with a real rather than imaginary or fantastic account of 'the life, sayings, deeds, sufferings and death' of Christ. If the Gospel writers could have said *anything* and still claim to be speaking of Jesus of Nazareth, if the so-called 'Easter experience' is compatible with any and every historical statement about this man, i.e. with no *historical* statement at all, then it seems to me meaningless to talk at all of a distinction between illusion and reality in the accounts of Christ given in the Gospels.

In the case of contemporary believers the significance of the historical content of faith is that it provides us with the concept of a focus for meditation. This in turn makes possible continuing growth of insight, and a continuing development in the understanding of the significance of this life and death. Further, a belief in these historical claims, and a belief that these are the *focus* of faith, are means of giving expression to the further belief that it is possible to know as men what is ultimately true about ourselves. This is so, inasmuch as we believe that what is ultimate or transcendent has been manifested in time, in a life and death. Consequently the Christian cannot claim that what is ultimately true about men and their God and what is ultimately important about human life must ever remain beyond their grasp, remain hidden. For that is precisely what the Christian believes has been manifested in the contingencies and vicissitudes of historical existence, and as such is in principle comprehensible to us.

None of this, however, should be taken to imply a longing

to return to the days of the 'old' quest for the historical Jesus. There are many reasons for not doing so. The first is historical scepticism bred by disagreements between competent and respected New Testament scholars. The second is the acceptance of the point made in different ways by both Tillich and Kierkegaard that historical enquiry cannot prove or verify faith. The third is that I have an alternative account of the relationship betwen history and faith, which will extend what has already been proposed as a partial answer to Fuchs's question about why it is that the Gospels do give such emphasis to recounting words and narrating incidents attributed to the historical Jesus.

Part of my answer to that question has already been given. The earliest witnesses clearly believed that my epistemological question about the status of the various witnesses required a distinction between objective and subjective accounts of what made the figure of Jesus decisive. Now it is already agreed that we cannot base the answer to that solely on historical evidence, but if the claims of witnesses are compatible with any and every belief about what the historical Jesus was like, then it seems that whatever the favoured witnesses or gurus say, would be true simply by virtue of their saying it. It is for this reason that I wish to stress the point that belief must be historically vulnerable. It is not conceivable that Caligula, Genghis Khan, or for different reasons Ronald Reagan could have the historical shape of the man who is for faith of 'decisive significance'. Consequently faith is committed to the view that whatever historical contours shape the life of Jesus, they cannot be identical to those which shape the lives of those three!

However, this takes us to the beginning of our search rather than its end, for I have no illusions about producing an agreed picture of Jesus and so solving our problem. In essence my answer to the question which Fuchs poses is that the fact that Jesus was an historical figure is what is of supreme significance. That historians and witnesses should disagree about even major elements of the interpretation of that life and death is, I shall argue, inevitable, and perhaps even essential. However, to avoid the risk of an extreme form of relativism, and indeed of relativism at all, we must agree that there are limits to how far disagreement and variation is tolerable. I have, by example, suggested where we might find some of these limits. The implication is that if historians did come to such a consensus, then they would *ipso facto* put faith at risk. In the next three chapters I shall try to show that the position which I am adopting is perhaps less simple-minded than might first appear.[11]

10

Goodness Incarnate?

In the last chapter I pointed out that questions of historicity are part of the broader question of what we are to make of the figure of Jesus. Inevitably, then, we find ourselves confronted by the whole battery of arguments and counter-arguments which constitute the subject-matter of Christology and which polarize on the doctrine of the incarnation. Clearly we are now swimming in deep waters and must look for markers which will provide an anchorage for philosophical enquiry.

Much of the philosophical interest in the idea of the incarnation focuses upon the problem of making sense of the claim that the attributes of an infinite and transcendent God might be found in a particular human being. Thus considerable insight as well as ingenuity is to be discovered in the writings of those who have addressed this problem and proposed a positive solution to it. What is equally noticeable is that there has been only limited discussion of what it might mean for perfect goodness to be made manifest in Jesus. Not surprisingly, this has been thought to be somewhat less of a difficulty for traditional Christology than the problems posed by the so-called metaphysical attributes of God.

My argument will be twofold: in the first place, I shall argue that the incarnation of perfect goodness is an idea which is no less problematic than any other transcendent attribute, albeit that the problems have a rather different character. In the second place, in this and the two chapters to follow I shall

offer an account of why it is that it is important that the
attempt to recount the words and narrate the deeds of the
historical Jesus should have been made. Thus in the context
of a discussion of the goodness of Jesus, I shall offer an
answer to the question posed by Ernst Fuchs. The starting
point, however, must be the issue of the manifestation in
particular form of perfect goodness.

Whatever the other difficulties which Plato faced in trying
to give an account of the relation between the Forms and
their particular instantiations, he did on the whole argue that
perfection or the ideal belonged to the universal or Form,
rather than to the individual or particular. The implications
of such a view for *Christian* theology are disturbing, for of
course, as Aquinas reminds us, 'It is clear that this man who
is Christ is a certain substance which is not universal but
particular';[1] and Aquinas devotes several chapters of his
Summa Contra Gentiles to the exploration of this belief. My
own intention is to focus upon one aspect of this, which
in post-Kantian theology has assumed a rather greater significance than it had for St Thomas, namely whether sense can
be attached to the idea of the manifestation of moral perfection in an individual or *particular* life and death. The route
which we shall follow will take us from Dostoevsky and
Kierkegaard, via Don Quixote, to contemporary Christological discussion.

In the winter of 1867/8 Dostoevsky's major literary
preoccupation was with the opening sections of his novel *The
Idiot*. We meet 'the idiot', the individual, on the first page of
the novel, returning from a long period of treatment in a
Swiss asylum to Moscow. The first description which we are
offered, is of a young man

> with very thick, fair hair, hollow cheeks, and a thin pointed
> and almost white little beard. His eyes were large, blue, and
> piercing, and there was something gentle but heavy in their
> look, something of that strange expression which makes
> people realize at first glance that they are dealing with an
> epileptic. The young man's face, however, was pleasant,
> sensitive, and lean, though colourless and at this particular
> moment, blue with cold.[2]

Shortly after his arrival in Moscow we are presented with a picture of the prince, Prince Myskhin, through the eyes of a servant of a rich Moscow family upon whom he calls:

> Although the prince was a simpleton – the servant had made up his mind about *that* – it seemed nevertheless improper to the general's valet to continue his conversation with a visitor, in spite of the fact that for some reason he could not help liking the prince – after his own fashion of course. But looked at from different point of view, the prince aroused in him a feeling of most violent indignation. (p. 45)

The novel tells of what befalls the prince in Moscow – and what befalls the Moscow visited by the prince – but it concludes with the prince's eventual return, or retreat, to his Swiss sanatorium. Dostoevsky's letters of that period tell a tale of literary audacity qualified by critical uncertainty. To his close friend, the poet Makov, he wrote, 'I have long been haunted by a certain idea, but I was afraid of making a novel out of it, because the idea is very difficult and I am not ready for it . . . This idea is – *to create a wholly beautiful character.* There can, in my opinion, be nothing more difficult than this . . . '[3] In a letter written on the next day to his niece Sofia, he made the explicit connection which has undoubtedly already occurred to you: 'The main idea of the novel is to present a positively beautiful human being . . . There is only one positively beautiful character in the world – Christ' (p. 164). The idea of beauty here is moral, rather than purely aesthetic, and indeed one translator has delineated Dostoevsky's problem as that of 'the representation of a truly perfect and noble man'.[4]

The difficulty facing Dostoevsky the novelist, is, in part, as he realized, the problem of incarnation – or at least one aspect of it. His comment on the fourth gospel contained in this same letter to his niece is a vivid illumination of his conception of the literary task upon which he was engaged: '. . . the appearance of this boundlessly infinite, beautiful person [Christ] is of course an infinite miracle in itself (the entire Gospel of St John is full of this thought: he finds the whole miracle in the incarnation alone, the manifestation of the beautiful).' It would be shortsighted indeed to dismiss this as piety tending towards sentimentality. It is, rather, the admiration of one writer for another. What Dostoevsky recognizes in the writer of the fourth gospel is what literary professionalism has taught him in one agonizing page after another: the manifestation of beauty, of moral perfection (for that is what he understands by beauty) is infinitely hard to achieve – 'the whole miracle', he agrees, is 'in the Incarnation alone, the manifestation of the beautiful'. It is the particularization of the beautiful, of goodness, indeed the very idea that goodness and beauty should be, or could be particularized (or 'incarnated'), which causes him to marvel.

This, of course, provides us with an important insight into Dostoevsky's understanding of what he was about in the creation of character, and specifically in his treatment of Prince Myshkin in *The Idiot*, of Sonia before that in *Crime and Punishment*, and of Zossima and Alyosha in *The Brothers Karamazov*. There may, however, be merit in reversing this pattern of enquiry and moving, not from the idea of incarnation to an understanding of Dostoevsky's compositional problems, but rather asking what light Dostoevsky's literary travails might shed upon the idea of incarnation, upon the idea of manifestation, and upon the process of particularization. Of course, this avenue of enquiry will produce, at most, a *partial* illumination of the issues, but I hope I shall not be accused of philosophical snideness if I suggest that theology these days might have reason to be thankful even for small mercies, and that a partial light from Dostoevsky might be worth several kilowatts of generation from more energetic, but less reflective, sources.

The theological issue is that of the notion of manifestation or particularization. In Christological terms this problem relates to the whole range of the attributes of divinity which, it is thought, might be made manifest in incarnation. Discussions of this have for obvious reasons focused upon the metaphysical attributes of the God of the philosophers – omniscience, omnipotence, omnipresence, and so on. One theme which has suffered neglect is the suggestion that the perfect goodness of God might somehow be made manifest in Christ. Certainly *one* aspect of this has been investigated thoroughly, namely the idea of the sinlessness of Christ, but what has escaped the attention of many is the fact that it is no easier to give an account of the particularization of perfect goodness than it is to clarify one's mind about the incarnation of omniscience or omnipotence. The Kantian account of this has exacerbated rather than solved the problem: for when he talks of attributing 'the archetype [of goodness] lying in our reason' to 'the Godman [on earth]', he is talking of Jesus of Nazareth as an *example* of goodness, rather than as the *incarnation* of goodness.

The issue is complex, and my proposal is that we might disentangle some of the strands involved by looking first at Dostoevsky's hesitation in the characterization of Myshkin. Dostoevsky's forebodings became, in retrospect, a judgement of his own failure. He clearly believed himself to have failed, and the most significant evidence of this is that within the year he was beginning to plan what was to become *The Brothers Karamazov*. When he started actually writing this novel, ten years later, he was still in pursuit of his literary dream of the portrayal of goodness and perfection. Although there too he failed, I do not think that the characters of Zossima and Alyosha are quite the disasters which some commentators would have us believe them to be. None the less, again, in his own terms, he was unsuccessful. Why should this be? I shall briefly review three different proposals on this matter.

According to some, even some of the sensitive interpreters, his failure in the end comes down to the fact that goodness, perfection, is dull, and that therefore the drama of evil in its various forms, which with such dazzling, yet insidious genius, stalk through Dostoevsky's novels, will inevitably set a literary standard which not even Dostoevsky himself can equal. Eliseo Vivas writes:

> But it cannot be denied that none of his saintly characters –

Sonia in *Crime and Punishment*, Myshkin and even Zossima – is endowed with as dense and authentic a humanity as his evil characters. Dostoevsky is aware of this criticism which it is not difficult to answer. The reason why they are not, is that genuine goodness and saintliness are harmonious, unassertive and hence undramatic, dull, affairs. But this is not a comment on them or on Dostoevsky, but upon us, his readers.[5]

Significantly, Dostoevsky does not offer the dullness of good people as an excuse for what he regarded as a literary failing. What this judgement fails to recognize is that for Dostoevsky the problem was not how to make goodness and perfection interesting; for that one might hope, as the pious often do, for a miracle in the character of the *reader*. The problem rather is that of portraying goodness or perfection at all: it is in the very manifestation, not in the heart of the reader, that a miracle is required. The problem is not how to make what is coherent interesting: it is how to find a coherent representation of what seems to defy delineation in particular form. What does the good man look like?

Other commentators have argued that Dostoevsky's 'saintly' characters lack 'reality', and that this implies a failure of technique; as if, by trying a little harder, Dostoevsky might have got it right. Dostoevsky would accept the negative side of this judgement. There is a common confession of failure which runs through his portrayal of Sonia, of Myshkin, of Zossima and of Alyosha. Murray Krieger, in his important book *The Tragic Vision*, makes the point in connection with Myshkin: 'There is Zossima as well as Alyosha in Myshkin. His retirement in the Swiss sanitorium both before and after the action of the novel is clearly his withdrawal from human involvement, his monastery where his modest sanctity goes its way in peace.'[6] The climax of the novel is the scene in which the prince is taken by his rival, Rogozhin, to the flat which Rogozhin shared with the woman whom both he and Myshkin loved – but each in their own way. Myshkin finds that Rogozhin has murdered Nastasya, and they sit in vigil as Rogozhin succumbs to a raging fever. The chapter concludes:

The prince was sitting motionless beside him on the cushions, and every time the sick man burst out screaming or began rambling, he hastened to pass his trembling hand gently over his hair and cheeks, as though caressing and soothing him. But he no longer understood the questions he was asked, and did not recognise the people who had come into his room and surrounded him. And if Schneider himself had come from Switzerland now to have a look at his former pupil and patient, remembering the condition in which the prince had been during the first year of his treatment in Switzerland, he would have given him up with a despairing wave of a hand and would have said, as he did then: 'An idiot!'[7]

And so the prince returns to the sanatorium. His goodness cannot withstand the continuing pressures of society, and it is, as such, less than perfect.

Did Dostoevsky simply fail to identify and individuate the right form of goodness? Again this is an over-simple reaction, for it omits to note the parallel way in which Sonia's goodness at the end of *Crime and Punishment* moves swiftly off-stage with its main task, the resurrection of the soul of Raskilnikov, as yet unaccomplished. Likewise in *The Brothers Karamazov*, Zossima defines the limited nature of his own goodness when he directs Aloysha to leave the monastery, to marry, and to live in commerce with, and in the constraint of, society at large. This was to be the central focus of the sequel volume to what we already have of *The Brothers Karamazov*. Significantly, it was never written. Once again the portrayal of goodness and perfection moves off-stage, and the manner of its manifestation escapes novelist and reader alike. The point is that in each case the conclusion of the novel is Dostoevsky's judgement upon his own characters. It seems as if goodness defies particularization.

Mochulsky's judgement on the matter is nearer the mark in that it implies that the failure here is not simply a failure of technique:

> The depiction of a 'positively beautiful individual' is a prodigious task. Art can approach it, but not solve it, for the beautiful individual is a saint. Sanctity is not a literary theme.

> In order to create the image of a saint, one has to be a saint oneself. Sanctity is a miracle; the writer cannot be a miracle-worker. Christ only is holy, but a novel about Christ is impossible.[8]

Again the negative force of this assessment is clear, but I cannot rest content with Mochulsky's account of what it means to claim that 'a novel about Christ is impossible', or to claim that 'sanctity is not a literary theme'. It is not that one has to be a saint in order to create the image of a saint. (The contrast between the life and the skills of many an artist denies the truth of that.) It is rather that there are inherent difficulties in the idea of 'the image of a saint' when, as for Dostoevsky, the image in question is that of perfect goodness, or the very idea of incarnation. Thus we see the inadequacies of three different attempts to give an account of Dostoevsky's failure to give particular form to his dream of 'a truly perfect and noble man'.

Perhaps a clue to the flaw in Dostoevsky's vision on this point can be found in his *Notebooks* for *The Idiot*, containing as they do constant interspersed references to the prince, to Christ, and – to Don Quixote. Mochulsky, indeed, refers to Myshkin as 'the Russian Don Quixote'. More explicit than the gnomic references to Quixote in the *Notebooks* is a further passage from Dostoevsky's letter to Sofia from which I have already quoted: '. . . of beautiful characters in Christian literature the most finished is Don Quixote. But he is beautiful only because he is at the same time ridiculous. Dickens' Pickwick (an infinitely weaker conception than Don Quixote but nevertheless immense) is also ridiculous and succeeds because of this.' (op. cit., p. 169) Dostoevsky's fascination with the portrayal of Quixote is both deep-seated and telling. Basically, he saw his own attempts to portray goodness as in the tradition of Cervantes' Don Quixote; and we know from his *Notebooks* for *The Brothers Karamazov* that ten years and more later he was still preoccupied with the fear that goodness in particular form will appear comic or ridiculous. In a letter written in 1879, he spoke of both his aim of offering

Zossima as a counterweight to Ivan the atheist, and also of
his forebodings:

> And here there was a further obligation of art: I had to present
> a modest but august figure, while life itself is full of the
> comic, and august only in its interior significance, so that in
> the biography of my monk I was forced willy-nilly, by the
> demands of art, to touch on the commonplace and the trivial,
> so as not to mar artistic realism.[9]

The fineness of judgement presupposed in Dostoevsky's
sense of marvel at the figure of Quixote is perhaps most
clearly delineated if we place alongside it the almost adjacent,
but obverse view of Kierkegaard:

> Don Quixote is the prototype for a subjective madness, in
> which the passion of inwardness embraces a particular finite
> fixed idea . . . In the type of madness which manifests itself as
> an aberrant inwardness, the tragic and the comic is that the
> something which is of such infinite concern to the
> unfortunate individual is a particular fixation which does not
> really concern anybody . . .[10]

Kierkegaard follows Dostoevsky's sense of the importance of
Quixote in European thought, but in the end he regards the
comic elements in Quixote as the outward form of the tragic
or even of the pathetic.

The difference between Dostoevsky and Kierkegaard on
this point, at one and the same time, marks out quite definitively two opposing conceptions of the manifestation of
goodness, and two divergent strands in contemporary
Christological debate. In exposition and justification of this
claim, I turn to a consideration of common elements in
Kierkegaard's *Purity of Heart* and *Concluding Unscientific Postscript*, both published in the early part of 1847.

For Kierkegaard, perfect goodness is what is given
expression in the title of his religious meditation *Purity of
Heart*. He, too, was preoccupied in his own way with the
nature of the manifestation or presence of 'purity of heart'.
Or again, despite his more than minimal admiration for the
ideals of the monastic life, Kierkegaard agreed with Dos-

toevsky that this could not be the definite setting for the expression or manifestation of goodness. This was not because he believed that goodness is less than perfect if it cannot be manifest and shown to survive outside the cloisters, but because he believed that there was no distinctive, definitive, external or particular form which goodness must take. Thus, whatever one makes of his detailed diagnosis of Don Quixote, it is clear that Kierkegaard was bound to find Quixote unsatisfactory, just as he will find *any* attempt to externalize and particularize goodness inadequate.

In the *Postscript* Kierkegaard argues that while it is true that every existing individual has a *telos*, there is no *external* distinctive expression of what this *telos* is. For all its difficulties, and the intellectual abuses to which it has since been subjected, his emphasis upon the hidden inward character of the ethical life is both important, and firmly-based in his account of the relationship between God and man. If God as eternal is absolutely different from man as temporal, then, he writes, '. . . an eternal happiness as the absolute good has the remarkable trait of being definable solely in terms of the mode of acquisition' (p. 382). Now, there are many diverse dimensions to this sort of remark, but I wish to restrict myself to two comments.

First, my interest here is in the negative implication that just as there is no adequate verbal expression of what eternal happiness, or relationship to God, as man's *telos* is, so there is no adequate distinctive outward expression of this. This leads Kierkegaard to the extreme conclusion that the individual (an ethical as well as a religious idea in Kierkegaard) '. . . is a stranger in the world of the finite, but does not manifest his heterogeneity, his separation from worldliness, by a foreign mode of dress. This would be a contradiction, since he would thereby qualify himself in a worldly manner' (p. 367). Or as he puts it elsewhere, the good man is not like the town mayor: he does not have a chain of office to help the rest of us identify him. 'He is incognito, but his incognito consists in having an appearance entirely like others.' (ibid.) There is no distinctive external form for the manifestation of man's telos or perfection.

My second comment is that this is in part a logical point which is being made. For Kierkegaard, the external or outer world is the world of finitude and temporality. To attempt to portray the absolute good in such a world is to give it an external, distinctive, particular, but inevitably limited form. A goodness which is thus limited is less than perfect. Perhaps this will lead us to ask whether it is clear what is being said when we talk of perfect goodness, and we shall have to consider the force of this question in due course.

If we turn briefly to *Purity of Heart*, we find Kierkegaard identifying 'purity of heart' with 'to will one thing'. Maddeningly, or perhaps even obtusely, he refuses to identify what that one thing is, other than in formal terms as 'to will the Good, as an individual, to will to hold fast to God'. There is no *single* identifiable external thing which is to be willed as *the* Good. Nor, alternatively, should we seek for many things which jointly constitute 'willing the Good'. One might well feel justified in regarding this as sheer perversity, but before that we ought to consider the context of these claims. What is Kierkegaard seeking to do in this work? He is *not* attempting to define what characterizes 'a truly perfect and noble man', nor to picture what purity of heart will look like. *Purity of Heart* is a meditation offered to be read before the act of confession. It is offered as a means of approach to self-examination and ultimately self-knowledge. It does this, however, not by presenting an image of what it is 'to will the Good', against which we may measure ourselves, finding ourselves deficient in this way or that: it offers, characteristically of Kierkegaard, a mirror which contains no image but our own, and this mirror, like the 'mirror on the wall', tells us the truth about ourselves.

Dostoevsky believed that it is intelligible to hope to present 'an image of goodness', 'a truly perfect and noble man'; Kierkegaard, on the other hand, denied that this is possible. Externally regarded, the good man, to the extent that he is good, travels incognito. Didactically, if one is to point a man towards goodness, one must do so by holding a mirror before him, which will cause him to pause and to reflect. In these ideas, of course, are foreshadowed two of the central preoccupations of twentieth-century Christological and theological thought – the incognito and self-knowledge.

Our starting point was the question of whether sense can be attached to the idea of the manifestation of moral perfection in an individual or particular life and death. The theological aspect of that is the idea of the incarnation of perfect goodness. We have considered Dostoevsky's struggles to portray just such perfection, literary struggles placed self-consciously within the context of the idea of incarnation. Despite his genius he failed. Kierkegaard offers, by implication, a critique of Dostoevsky's Promethean labours. His failure was inevitable since goodness has no external particular form.

What, then, of christology? The discussion upon which we have been engaged in this chapter indicates two very different paths which might be followed in our approach to the question of the nature of the goodness of Jesus, or to the question of the manner of the manifestation of goodness presupposed in the idea of incarnation. Dostoevsky failed in Myshkin, and in subsequent attempts, to particularize perfect goodness: Kierkegaard believed that the only external or particular expression of goodness which will not distort reality is the incognito of hiddenness, and that although we can be interrogated by goodness, it will only be as a mirror interrogates those who pause to consider what they see reflected in it.

There have been those whose Christology has been preoccupied with the quest, or even the new quest for the historical Jesus, who have been preoccupied with discovering the particular form in which the goodness of Jesus was manifest. A complementary preoccupation has often been, therefore, the sinlessness of Jesus. Is the failure of the historical quest, and of the debate about sinlessness to produce positive conclusions, however, not simply a lack of evidence, which in an ideal world could be overcome? If we accept the legitimacy of Dostoevsky's hope of 'representing a truly perfect and noble man', then that is so. But if we are persuaded by Kierkegaard's arguments, then the historical quest was in that respect bound to fail. A historical picture of goodness incarnate is a confusion of ideas.

The quest was bound to result in the sorts of conclusions drawn most strikingly, perhaps, in Bonhoeffer's lectures on Christology. There one finds a concentration upon the incognito or historical ambiguity of the life of Jesus. He argues that part of the truth about Jesus is that 'He was not the perfectly good man,' although he does quickly modify this to read, 'He did things which *outwardly* sometimes look like sin.'[11] (my italics) Again, in Kierkegaardian terms, it is not simply that we do not have enough historical evidence to clarify the picture. The point is that the Individual '. . . is a stranger in the world of the finite, but does not manifest his heterogeneity, his separation from worldliness, by a foreign mode of dress.' And, of course, this applies equally to Jesus, as to any other. The particularization of goodness is essentially an inward matter.

My argument has been that in the end the attempt to give a picture, whether historical or otherwise, of the manifestation of perfect goodness is based upon a confusion. None the less, to affirm this is not to affirm that perfect goodness was not made manifest in particular historical form: it is to make a point which if true is important, about the nature of goodness and about the manner of its manifestation. It will be my argument in the subsequent chapters that a particularly appropriate and perhaps even unique way to reveal this truth demands that the historicity of the figure of Jesus is accorded a central significance. In the terms used in chapter 9, the historicity of the figure of Jesus is in one clear sense internally related to the answer to the question asked by all Christologies including that of Ogden.[12]

11

Is Jesus Unique?

Jesus and his disciples set out for the villages of Caesarea
Philippi. On the way he asked his disciples, 'Who do men say
I am?' They answered, 'Some say John the Baptist, others
Elijah, others one of the prophets.' 'And you,' he asked, 'who
do you say I am?' Peter replied: 'You are the Messiah.' Then
he gave them strict orders not to tell anyone about him; and
he began to teach them that the Son of Man had to undergo
great sufferings, and to be rejected by the elders, chief priests,
and doctors of the law: to be put to death, and to rise again
three days afterwards. He spoke about it plainly. (Mark 8.27–
32)

This passage sets the theological question clearly before us. Is
he 'one of the prophets' or is he someone or something quite
other? Of course we know, or at least have been taught to
know by the development of the critical study of the Scriptures, that even this earliest of the gospels is written after the
event, and that the attribution of Jesus of what seem to be
detailed forebodings about the manner of his death may well
represent a reconstruction based as much on 'what-he-must-
have-said/meant' as on accurate recollection and reporting.
None the less, even someone as radical in his approach as
Ogden accepts the centrality, for the development of
Christianity, of this passage and the question which it sets.
Neither Christian belief nor Christian theology can long
evade it, and of course it does constitute a particular test-case
for one who adopts the standpoint of revisionary theology.

The question of the uniqueness of Jesus might arise in many contexts other than those provided by Christian theology and Christian belief. Most obviously it arises in the context of an awareness and study of other religious traditions. Here again, it is clear that there are many different aspects to the question. For example within the Islamic tradition Jesus is recognized as 'one of the prophets', but as of less significance than Muhammad. Within Buddhism there is room for as many as truly teach and follow the eightfold path based on the four noble truths. Perhaps we should take warning and avoid asking in general terms whether Jesus is unique, and try to ask some more specific questions about Jesus and Muhammad or Jesus and Siddhārtha Gautama. There is some sense in this, but two factors incline me against it for the time being. The first is that if one is to engage in an enquiry as to whether the Christian tradition can be accommodated within the contours of this revisionary theology, then one must first ask the question of the confession which focuses upon the figure of Jesus. The second point is that there are some general comments about the notion of uniqueness which will serve as useful prolegomana to the rest of the discussion.

The idea of uniqueness belongs to a clutch of very fragile notions which are often used in the expression of religious belief, but which run the risk of being classed as either hyperbole or nonsense: other examples include talk of the 'absolute otherness' of God or of the radically 'qualitative difference' between God and man. If the uniqueness of Jesus is construed after either of those expressions, then problems of a major order will confront us.

If, for example, we try to think of God as the early Barth did, as 'wholly other', the following difficulty arises: how can we know, think, believe, conceive, or even imagine anything whatsoever about a God who is wholly other? If he is other in this respect or that, we may well begin to believe, or conceive or whatever, but if he is *wholly* other, we can think or say nothing about him whatsoever. Such terms as 'absolutely' or 'wholly' should be seasoned with a pinch of hyperbolic salt. To an Aborigine transported in the space of a few hours from his 'humpy' in the desert regions of the northern Territory to the centre of Sydney, it may seem appropriate to describe Sydney as 'absolutely' different, or 'wholly' other. But far apart as these locations and styles of life are, they are only *relatively* different if one is to be pedantically literal. This example alone should be sufficient warning against the tendency of absolute differences or even notions of uniqueness to slip over the horizon of intelligibility.

There is a comparable point to be made about the uniqueness of Jesus. If it is the uniqueness of absolute difference, its significance is either purely negative or non-existent. If Jesus, or anyone else for that matter, is to be regarded as unique, it must be in respect of this property or that capacity. Now if this analysis is correct, certain important deductions can be made. The first is that the starting point for this way of thinking is the humanity of Jesus. It is being assumed that Jesus is distinct from other men in some ultimately significant manner, but that there is much that he shares with them. The very posing of the question and the way in which it is posed presuppose that in important respects Jesus shared the common lot of humanity.

One way of understanding this – which is of immense significance for these questions – was foreshadowed in chapter 9 in the quoted sumary of Troeltsch's three principles. The second and third of these are particularly relevant in that they pose a central question about how we might understand the solidarity which Jesus has with other human beings:

> (2) the principle of analogy, by which he [Troeltsch] meant that we are able to make such judgements of probability only if we presuppose that our own present experience is not radically dissimilar to the experience of past persons; and (3) the principle of correlation, by which he meant that the phenomena of man's historical life are so related and interdependent that no radical change can take place at any one point in the historical nexus without effecting a change in all that immediately surrounds it.[1]

The question which these principles pose for us is whether a human being girt around with these restrictions of historicity could ever be sufficiently unique to play the role which a Christian response to the question 'Who do you say that I am?' seems to demand.

The risk is that in so confining the figure of Jesus through emphasis on his humanity and consequent historicity, we have restricted his uniqueness or difference to a uniqueness which each human has. I refer here to the fact – important as it is to our account of the identity of persons through time – that each of us has a unique spatio-temporal location, and that this is a sufficient condition of the possibility of the attribution of identity through time, for each of us traces a single unique path through space and time. This, however, is hardly adequate to a conception of the uniqueness of Jesus which would serve the needs of faith.

The difficulty which we face here is comparable to the general problem which has faced all of those who have attempted to give an account of the relationship between history and faith: either we stress what is objective and so run the risk of not even approaching the question of what is central to faith, or we appeal to what is essentially subjective and run the risk of imagining what we want to be, rather than believing what is. In this case the danger is that either we restrict ourselves to a form of uniqueness shared by each and every human being, or we attempt to make the figure of Jesus so (absolutely) different that (in the end) we can only say what he is *not* like, again leaving open the question whether we are saying anything at all. As long as we agree that our starting point is a human figure, however, we do at least have a beginning which can be anchored in reality, and I do regard the historicity which is part of the human lot as in principle the means of escaping a purely subjective Christology.

The question of what one means or might mean by uniqueness is intimately bound up with the question of what one accepts as possible. For example there are two very strong traditions within Christianity which would each solve the problem of uniqueness in a very clear way. (They would each, of course, have serious attendant problems of their own, but enough of that till later.) The first of these derives uniqueness from the unusual circumstances of Jesus' birth, and is given expression in the creed thus: 'born of the Virgin Mary'. The second tradition stems from the circumstances surrounding his death and finds expression in the words 'and on the third day he rose again'.

Now there are many comments to be made about these traditions, but I shall restrict myself to those most central to the theme of this book. In the first place the uniqueness which these traditions propose may be the result of twentieth-century ignorance, for the idea of parthogenesis is not unique to Christanity. The most significant statement in European thought outside the Christian tradition which combines Messianism with reference to one born of a 'maid' ('virgo') is to be found in Virgil's fourth ('Messianic') *Eclogue*:

> Lo, the last age of Cumae's seer has come!
> Again the great millennieal æon dawns.
> Once more the hallowed Maid appears, once more
> King Saturn reigns, and from high heaven descends
> The firstborn child of promise. Do but thou,
> Pure Goddess, by whose grace on infant eyes
> Daylight first breaks, smile softly on this babe;
> The age of iron in his time shall cease
> And golden generations fill the world.[2]

In the second place such 'supernatural' solutions to the problem will be bought at a very great price, for they put the most essential elements of Jesus' life (at least the most important elements on *their* principles) beyond the horizons of historical enquiry. The second and third of Troeltsch's principles are clearly set aside by each of these ways of construing the uniqueness of Jesus. Evidently the principle of analogy no longer applies for what is proposed is precisely that what is unique about Jesus is what is so radically dissimilar to our own experience that it lies outside of history, and arguably falsifies the claim to humanity made on his behalf. The third principle offered by Troeltsch is equally set aside for it demands complete enmeshment within the causal nexus of historical events. The doctrine of the virgin birth and the belief in the physical resurrection of Jesus are each ways of removing him from the net of history in one way or another. (For example, if we take the resurrection stories literally, and such a possibility cannot be ruled out a priori, then we still have the difficulty of accounting for what then happened to the body, without postulating what is unintelligible, namely a non-historical event.)

The final point which I want to make about these two ways of giving an account of the uniqueness of Jesus is that they are not open to me for quite other reasons. I have already indicated that my premisses are those of the revisionary theology of natural religion, and that this rules out the possibility of appeal to special or supernatural revelation. Now if these events are in some clear sense beyond the natural, knowledge of them or grounds or occasion for belief in them would have to be derived from some such supernatural source. If there are those who wish to construct their theology on such a basis, then so be it, but I dance to another drum.

There are two rather different possible ways of giving an account of the uniqueness of Jesus, each of which has had its supporters within the Christian tradition, and each of which can have two differing but complementary forms. The variations involved have each had a history which has given them more varying degrees of prominence at one time, while at another perhaps banished them to fideistic borderlands, as intellectual fashions have altered.

The uniqueness of Jesus has at times been attached to a particular account of his deeds. The most obvious candidate here is the whole corpus of biblical material known as 'the miracle stories'. A classic statement which exemplifies the view to which I am pointing is to be found in Alan Richardson's *The Miracle-Stories of the Gospels*.[3] The opening sentence sets the tone:

> The miracle-stories form an essential and inseparable part of
> the Gospel tradition, and their aim, like that of every other
> part of the tradition, is to deepen the understanding of the
> mystery of Who Jesus is and to set forth the implications of
> this recognition for the whole life and conduct of those who
> seek to follow Him.

Now there are many points here which ought to be
examined, including the ambiguity of the capitalized 'Gospel'
tradition, but I must restrict myself to those central to the
concerns of this book.

Richardson rightly wants to preserve the historicity of
Jesus and therefore the role of historical criticism in the
evaluation of all claims about him and his life including the
miracle-stories. With this I agree, but where we must part is
in his insistence that these stories lie at least very near the
heart of our answer to the question of who Jesus is: 'The
miracle-stories as an essential part of the preaching of apostolic Christianity, confront us with the question whether the
power of God was or was not revealed in the person and
work of Jesus Christ. They compel us to say Yes or No' (p.
126). I have three reasons for not following the same theological path as Richardson. In the first place I have started from a
very different position: whereas Richardson clearly belongs
to that school of theologians whose intention is to do full
justice to every element of the tradition which they inherit
from their theological forebears, I have rather happily agreed
that in trying to define a modern account of natural religion I
must inevitably select from within the inherited tradition
those elements which such an approach can recognize and
deal with. (In mitigation I point out that even the most
hardened traditionalist must admit that such a sifting has
taken place in the very formation of the tradition, and that
elements which were regarded as quite central in earlier
periods are now given at most a peripheral place – for
example there is remarkably little serious discussion of the
figure of Satan, or of the idea of Hell, whereas at one time no
self-respecting preacher could possibly exclude these from
public utterance.)

The second reason for being unable to follow Richardson is that the conception of 'the power of God' imlicit in his work is simply incompatible with all that I have already written in chapters 2 and 4 on the question of God. In the absence of good reasons for recanting, it would be quite wrong to try to have my theological cake and crumble it. Although neither of these points would initially carry much weight with Richardson, a third reason for rejecting appeal to the miracle-stories as grounds for talk of the uniqueness of Jesus to which he would have to pay attention is that the idea of a miracle-worker was one which had common currency in that period. There were certainly others of whom this claim was made and concerning whom the question of unique significance did not arise. Perhaps this is one of the reasons why in some cases the miracle-stories are accompanied by stories of Jesus insisting that the disciples keep silent about them. Perhaps these stories pander too much to the tastes of those who seek after a sign. There are other difficulties of a more general nature which apply to other accounts of the unique significance, and I shall reserve discussion of them until we have looked at some alternatives to Richardson.

One tradition which gained considerable momentum in the eighteenth and nineteenth centuries amongst those who focused upon the deeds of Jesus as the location of his unique-ness, is that of referring to the example of Jesus. This does not confine itself to contemplating one or two particular acts or deeds, but refers to the whole life of Jesus as a definitive example of goodness. Kant has given an unnervingly clear account of this view. It is unnerving in that its very clarity shows its inadequacy. He refers to the 'ideal of moral perfec-tion', and 'this archetype of the moral disposition in all its purity'. Such an idea or ideal

> of a humanity pleasing to God (hence of such moral perfec-tion as is possible to an earthly being who is subject to wants and inclinations) we can represent to ourselves only as the idea of a person who would be willing not merely to dis-charge all human duties himself and to spread about him goodness as widely as possibly by precept and example, but

even, though tempted by the greatest allurements, to take
upon himself every affliction, up to the most ignominious
death, for the good of the world and even for his enemies.[4]

Kant's argument is that the personification of the archetype
of such goodness is the only adequate means of generating
the strength necessary to undergo such a testing of moral
conviction and to 'remain true to [our] exemplar'.

This may well be true, although in view of the content of
the previous chapter, I should have to modify the
formulation of it considerably. However, even if we leave
that point aside for the moment, Kant's clarity about the
implications of this is instructive: 'We need . . . no empirical
example to make the idea of a person morally well-pleasing
to God our archetype: this idea as an archetype is already
present in our reason' (p. 56). There is no room here for more
than a good philosophical example. Such an example, where
the form of goodness is clothed in the literary trappings of
flesh and blood, is perhaps of inspirational or even pedagogic
value, but in terms of the insights there is no need for this
example, for it is *only* an example of what could quite independently be thought even if not so well expressed. If the
example is not necessary even at a literary or fictional level,
even less is it necessary to affirm that this man existed, let
alone that he might be 'supernaturally begotten'. Thus,
whatever value the figure of Jesus may be as an example, that
he can play this role cannot provide a basis for claiming that
he is of unique significance.

There are further problems about viewing Jesus as an
example of 'ideal moral perfection' who is 'willing to dis-
charge all human duties'. On the one hand it is not clear from
the accounts which we have what duties he believed himself
to have to his parents and his family, let alone whether he
discharged them. On the other, as we discovered in the
previous chapter, the idea of moral perfection in incarnate or
particular form is itself a very difficult one.

Amongst those who have seen something of the problems
of seeking Jesus' uniqueness in his deeds, an alternative

strategy which has gained some currency is to emphasize the role of Jesus as teacher rather than exemplar. Thus, it might be argued, Jesus will be seen to be of unique significance when we see what is uniquely distinctive about his teaching. This proposal must be evaluated in the light of two types of criticism. The first point is that if what is unique about Jesus is his teaching, we have a strange paradox. At best he seems to have taught in such a way that important elements in his teaching were misunderstood by the disciples and followers to whom he entrusted such teaching: at worst he simply was mistaken about when the second coming was to be. Undoubtedly one of the most difficult tasks facing the early church must have been the acceptance of the fact that the apocalyptic vision of the second coming was not to be realized in their lifetime.

The second point about laying the emphasis upon teaching is more subtle and has been most eloquently expressed by Kierkegaard. As Kierkegaard argues, the most important thing about a teacher is what he teaches. Indeed as Socrates consistently argued, the teacher must be set on one side so that what is taught may be absorbed. Whether we use the Socratic metaphor of the midwife or the Kierkegaardian suggestion that the teacher is at most the 'occasion' of learning, the implications are clear:

> From the standpoint of Socratic thought every point of departure in time is *eo ipso* accidental, an occasion, a vanishing moment. The Teacher himself is no more than this. . . The Socratic principle holds, that the Teacher is merely an occasion whoever he may be, even if he is God.[5]

It is worth noting in passing that this is quite consonant with Buddhist thought. Stated in this fashion Kierkegaard's point is well nigh irresistible. His own way of dealing with it is to distinguish between providing the occasion of learning, and providing the conditions necessary for learning.

This is a very important distinction, but I do not share with Kierkegaard the construction which he puts upon it. He stresses that if the moment of time, the occasion of learning, is to have decisive significance, that can only be because the teacher is more than the occasion of learning, that he somehow makes learning possible. The assumption must then be that in this particular case of teaching and learning the teacher must add something decisive to what is learnt, so that he – the teacher – is of more than accidental significance. In positing how or what this might be, Kierkegaard leans towards the possibility that there is something in man which prevents the learning in question. The decisive role of the teacher is to remove this barrier by creating within the learner the condition necessary for understanding the truth:

> What now shall we call such a Teacher, one who restores the lost condition and gives the learner the Truth? Let us call him *Saviour*, for he saves the learner from his bondage and from himself; let us call him *Redeemer*, for he redeems the learner from the captivity into which he had plunged himself . . .
>
> Such a Teacher the learner will never be able to forget. For the moment he forgets him he sinks back again into himself. (pp. 21–2)

In this way Kierkgaard argues that the teach is of decisive significance. There are some elements which I should like to pick up from this, but I shall first have to sketch out the very different context of the end of this chapter and develop its implications into the next one. The initial point of present concern is that Kierkegaard has helped show why the idea of the teaching of Jesus is not adequate to the provision of an account of the unique significance of Jesus. Kierkegaard's suggestion that we might find something in the notion of our ability to respond to the teaching is an important one and we shall return to it. However, rather than leaning towards stressing some inadequacy in the learner as the key to this, I shall concentrate on the nature of what it is that has to be learned or understood.

To summarize, we have briefly considered a battery of suggestions as to how we may give a possible account of the unique significance of jesus. For one reason or another none of these has proved adequate. In addition to the individual

points raised about each of these cases, there is one general
point which applies to them all. On the one hand each of
these accounts presupposes a particular reading of the life of
Jesus considered historically. Thus, for example, one of these
accounts presupposes that particular (miracle-) stories are
true. (To be fair to Alan Richardson he, for one, does in
general terms accept that the implications of this are to give a
place to historical criticism, but he does not discuss in detail
just how this will work out if there is a clash between faith
and historical enquiry.) The problem here is that as we have
already noted, there is little agreement to be found between
specialist scholars about the historical content of the life of
Jesus beyond the barest of bare outlines. To be too closely
attached to particular historical details is to be crucially at risk
to the ebb and flow of historical research.

One option open to us would be to discard completely the
idea of the unique significance of Jesus. I do not propose to
do this for I believe that there is one possible account open to
a proponent of a revisionary theology such as this one. I shall
spend the rest of this chapter and the whole of the next
outlining and defending that account.

The first step must be to draw a distinction between showing the notion of unique significance to be intelligible in this
context, and demonstrating that this description is truly
applicable to Jesus. I believe that I can succeed in the first of
these, but the second is a very complex matter indeed.

The next stage of my argument must be to rehearse the
constraining factors which the argument so far has placed on
any candidate for the status of giving an account of the
unique significance of Jesus. The three main constraints are as
follows:

(1) as just noted, an account of the unique significance of
    Jesus which depends upon a particular and detailed
    historical reconstruction of aspects of his life is so
    vulnerable as to be unacceptable;
(2) any account of the unique significance of Jesus must
    none the less give to the figure of Jesus, rather than to,

for example, his teaching, a particular and essential
role;

(3) in the interests of avoiding a relativizing subjectivity,
any such role must still retain the centrality and
importance of the historical Jesus, or in the terms of
chapter 9, I do not wish to abandon the claim that the
historicity is internally related to the faith.

On a first reading, it might well be thought that I have
simply and completely established the impossibility of the
task which I have set myself, by listing three conditions
whose respective fulfilments are incompatible.

Indeed it is the *prima-facie* difficulty of meeting and
reconciling all of these conditions which has driven many to
discount the importance of retaining the historical figure of
Jesus as central to their Christology. Ogden, for example,
offers a Christology and an account of the uniqueness of Jesus
which satisfy the first two of these conditions, but which, as
we have seen, reject the third as unimportant. Thus he argues
that the important affirmations made about Jesus include the
'existential–historical', but not the 'empirical–historical'. The
role of critical history is protected, but it is limited to enquiry
into the testimony of the earliest believers. The questions
asked do not include discussion of whether the testimony of
the earliest witnesses is confirmed or otherwise by what may
be known of the historical. This may avoid all the problems
posed by disagreement between the specialists, and the risks
of historical vulnerability, but it does so at the price of
espousing a form of subjectivity.

My bold, perhaps foolhardy claim is that an account of the
uniqueness of Jesus can be developed which holds fast to all
three constraining principles. The chief difficulty which must
be faced is that of reconciling the need to avoid the details of
an historical reconstruction which seem only to launch belief
into the arena of the disputes and uncertainties of the
historico-critical method, and the demand that none the less
the historicity of Jesus must be retained as central. My proposal will be that we can reconcile these apparent opposites by

first distinguishing between historicity *per se*, and a detailed or even general historical picture. In essence this distinction has been foreshadowed in the chapter on historicity and faith. In the next chapter I shall examine this distinction further, arguing both that it is compatible with the stance of my revisionary theology, and that it can give a clear and theologically significant account of what it means to affirm that Jesus is unique.

12

Grounds for Optimism?

At the end of the previous chapter I committed myself to giving an account of the unique significance of Jesus in a context which is subject to three prima-facie incompatible constraints. These were:

(1) an account of the unique significance of Jesus which depends upon a particular and detailed historical reconstruction of aspects of his life is so vulnerable as to be unacceptable;

(2) any account of the unique significance of Jesus must none the less give to the figure of Jesus, rather than to, for example, his teaching, a particular and essential role;

(3) in the interests of avoiding a relativizing subjectivity any such role must still retain the centrality and importance of the historical Jesus, or in the terms of chapter nine, I do not wish to abandon the claim that the historicity is internally related to the faith.

The argument of this chapter is that it is possible to give such a relatively tradition account and that in so doing I shall be helped rather than hindered by the comparatively radical and negative departure points of my revisionary theology.

There will be two main elements to my argument: the first will be the elaboration of a formal distinction between referring to the historicity of Jesus *per se* and referring to the historicity of particular claims made about the deeds or words of Jesus. I shall argue that it is because we have overlooked the importance of the former, historicity *per se*, that we have overemphasized the anxieties of trying to establish the latter, the historicity of particular claims about the deeds or words of Jesus. The second main element of my argument will be the examination of an analysis of the 'work' of Jesus (to use the traditional theological term) in terms of the concepts of optimism and hope.

I have already argued (chapter 9) that the notion of historicity in itself as applied to Jesus is of considerable theological importance. In advance of the discussion of any detailed point of historical fact about the life and times of Jesus, the very claim that he was an historical person is itself of major theological significance. Most importantly, historicity in itself retains in central position the idea of some element of objectivity in accounts of Jesus and in the assessment of them. It gives sense to the possibility of setting limits to what faith can be, to what can be said of Christ and God: the idea that accounts of Jesus, whether those of the earliest known witnesses or of contemporary believers, can be nearer or further from the truth can be given clear sense (cf. the fifth of my criteria outlined in chapter 1), all this from the notion of historicity *per se*. One consequence of this, of course, is that the claims of belief are in principle open to possible falsification, but this is a price which is unavoidable if we are to insist upon some element of objectivity in our account of Jesus.

It will be apparent that my account of Jesus is less at risk than those accounts which depend upon constructing or reconstructing a detailed picture of the life or words of Jesus. The substantial difficulties over reaching agreement on the latter have persuaded not only the faint-hearted, but even some fairly self-confident historians that the aim of historicity in our Christology is itself misguided. Certainly any answer by twentieth-century theologians to the question 'Who do you say that I am?', which depends upon detailed and specific historical, claims, is *ipso facto* deeply vulnerable to falsification. My claims are much more modest and to that extent much less vulnerable, though there is still here a residual unclarity to which I must return in due course. It will be more helpful, however, to give an account of the historical vulnerability of my picture after I have introduced and discussed the other main element of my argument – the analysis of the 'work' of Jesus through the concepts of hope and optimism.

The notion of the 'work' of Jesus, pointed to by Anselm's question 'Cur Deus Homo?', has always been a difficult one to handle, and for someone who is following the grail of the revisionary theology of natural religion, it must appear to all intents and purposes unmanageable. But my argument will be that this is appearance rather than reality, for there is a potentially clear account on my principles which can be given of the idea of the work of Jesus. It will not require reference to dubious transactions between God and whoever else; nor will it involve reference to non-natural or supernatural events. On the other hand we do not need to flee to the subjectivities of a 'work' which is to be understood wholly and only as a change of attitude or awareness within the believer, though there is no reason why it should exclude the latter.

The notion of the 'work' of Jesus, the idea that Jesus achieved something, is internally related to the idea that such a man existed. It is only temporal (i.e. historical) beings who *do* things. Fictional characters do not *do* or achieve things (apart from within their unreal or fictional world), although the author who creates them may, by so doing, himself do or bring about something. There is here an important theological distinction between the work of Jesus and, in another quite different sense, the 'work' of the earliest recorders of the tradition about Jesus. I wish to retain this distinction and to do this I must give some account of what Jesus did or achieved.

What on my account the historical Jesus did or achieved – this work – was to make possible the hope and belief which itself makes possible the rejection of radical pessimism in favour of a form of optimism. It is a difficult and arduous business to give an account of this, but when that has been done the content of the belief can, I think, be clearly presented.

If the work of Jesus is to show how hope and belief are possible, then the first thing that must be asserted is that the form or manner of this showing must be related to the content of what is shown. Thus my argument will attempt to establish that the content of that hope and belief which can ultimately banish radical pessimism will have as its appropriate expression the life, sayings, deeds and death of a man who lived subject to the vicissitudes of history. In order to achieve that conclusion I must first elaborate just what is involved in the rejection of radical forms of pessimism. You must excuse me if I seem to follow too closely here the negative side of my intention by speaking of 'the *rejection* of radical forms of *pessimism*', rather than more positively of establishing grounds for *optimism*. The reason for this is neither the traditional dourness of my race, nor an attempt to reach the legendary heights of bleakness set by Ingemar Bergmann! It is simply a wariness of the charge of simple-mindedness which seems to be levelled almost by automatic reflex at any mention of the word 'optimism'. One who earns his living by lecturing inevitably feels vulnerable at Gabriel Marcel's jibe that 'an optimist is essentially a maker of speeches'.[1] Whether this charge is appropriate is not ultimately important, but the claim coupled with it lies very near the centre of the modern European *psyche*, and as such as, if true, very important as well as damning to my whole enterprise. 'Perhaps such thing as a deep optimist does not exist.' The debasement of the term 'optimist' signalled in that remark – towards which one feels sympathetically drawn–is reason enough for parsimony in the use of the word 'optimism' until its potential for describing non-superficial outlooks has been established. Only then perhaps will it be of service in elaborating an account of the significance of Jesus.

A *bon mot* on the subject by J.B. Cabell will help us to raise a fundamental question about the distinction between optimism and pessimism: 'The optimist proclaims that we live in the best of all possible worlds; and the pessimist fears that this is so.' Is the difference between optimist and pessimist a difference in empirical beliefs about how things are? At one level this is so. For example, one may be optimistic or pessimistic about the state of the economy, or about the likelihood of nuclear war in the present decade. In either of these cases it might well be that the difference in outlook is in the end an expression of difference in empirical beliefs about fuel costs, or the intentions of the USSR in South-East Europe. Important though such issues are, I am not at all persuaded that 'metaphysical' or 'theological' optimism is of this form, and the point worth preserving in Cabell's remark is that the optimist and the pessimist might well not disagree about the empirical facts, nor about what inferences may be drawn from the facts.

The reaction of some to such a view is that optimism and pessimism must therefore be a matter of 'attitudes' to the facts, rather than belief about the facts. Difficult though it may be, this reaction must be resisted for it too easily divides human responses into the cognitive and the non-cognitive, with religious belief being implausibly trimmed to fit the former mould, or dismissively poured into the latter. In either case, I suggest, a distortion results, but in order to show that this is so, I shall have to try to give a less misleading picture of both optimism and pessimism.

The first and most important step is to recognize that in this area we are dealing with what might be called the triumph of good over evil. What I have referred to as 'metaphysical' optimism or pessimism is a difference between those who in some sense believe in the triumph of good, and those who reject such a claim. Now what sense can be given to such a claim? There are, I believe, three different positive ways of trying to give an answer to this question. For reasons which will become partially apparent, I shall concentrate on the third of these.

Firstly, a classical picture of the triumph of good over evil is one which concentrates on the future. The essence of the belief, whether utopian or eschatological, is that there will be a time when the vision of a just or pure society will be realized. There has been at times an over-hasty rejection of this (in so far as it was tied to an idea of progress), sometimes, it seems, at the behest of a weary indulgent cynicism, rather than as a result of genuine realism. On the other hand, whatever the value of vision in human choice (and the value should not be underestimated), there are illusions involved in the idea of the perfectibility of finite creatures which require and merit detailed examination. Perhaps it is because of these that there is a continuing fascination with the idea of infinite time being required or available for the purification of the soul. Two very different interpretations of this view are to be found in Kant's argument for the immortality of the soul, and in Hick's view of the moral development of the human person as expressed in *Death and Eternal Life*.[2] Thus these versions of optimism and pessimism include beliefs either in the capacities of human beings for moral progress within human history, or the non-finitude of the human soul or person, and correlated moral potential. As Kant was well aware, they also include either beliefs about the providential ordering of the cosmos, or, as at present, a belief, on whatever grounds, that what Presidential advisers from time to time envisage in their 'worst-case' scenarios will not interrupt our painstaking moral growth.

The difficulties inherent in the idea that the grounds for hope are in large part the grounds for belief in a life to come raise rather different problems which I have discussed elsewhere.[3]

A second form of the distinction between optimism and pessimism can be given by looking towards the past. Thus optimism would be justified because goodness has in some definitive way been realized. The strong version of this, allied to some forms of belief in the incarnation, is that in some sense, in the life and death of Jersus of Nazareth, absolute or perfect goodness has taken human, particular form. The weaker version is that we have known of good acts whose goodness is undeniable, which can be attributed to men and women whom we regard as good.

I have much sympathy with both of these ways of regarding the issue, but as we have already seen, I also have reservations. In the stronger case, there is much work still to be done in specifying the sense in which it is believed to be true that Jesus of Nazareth is goodness incarnate in particular form, and I shall return to this in due course. In the weaker case, the issue is still unclear between two different possibilities. At worst one might well still have in mind some form of calculus in which one weighs good acts against bad. It is enough to say that there is no acceptable way of constructing such a calculus. Alternatively one might, in a prima facie implausible way, be arguing that one good act, or one good man, is sufficient justification for optimism. Despite the apparent preciousness of such a view it has much to be said for it, but its depth can only be seen by ceasing to regard it as dependent for its intelligibility upon what has happened in the near or distant past.

Likewise, in order to elucidate the significance of the incarnation, for the stronger version, we must transfer our discussion from concern with what is, to what may be, from actuality to possibility.

In the end, the account which I wish to give of the distinction between optimism and pessimism, is that it is a distinction between those who regard goodness as a human *possibility*, and those who deny this. Such a view of optimism may seem to be distinctly attenuated, but I shall argue that it is not, and I shall further argue that the philosophical and theological issues of ultimate significance in this area receive their best and clearest focus through this particular conceptual lens.

The issue between the optimist and the pessimist is ultimately the issue of whether goodness is a possibility. Such a formulation may be understood in a number of ways, but I shall concentrate upon talking of human goodness. The Psalmist asks, 'What is man that thou art mindful of him?' One answer, an answer which the radical or metaphysical pessimist cannot share, is that man is a creature for whom goodness is a possibility. The point then is, what sense can be attached to such a claim? There are two different but complementary ways of formulating this question:

(1) The difference between optimist and pessimist might be seen as a difference in view about what human beings do or can achieve;

(2) The difference between optimism and pessimism is a difference about the intelligibility of the claim that goodness is a human possibility.

(1) Stated in this way, we might seem once again to be disagreeing about a straightforwardly empirical matter. Although empirical beliefs do certainly form one of the elements which constitute optimism and pessimism, the nature of the role which they play is complex. The complexity will begin to define itself if we consider the ways in which (1) might be denied.

(a) One form of denial is to argue that the nature of goodness is such that it presupposes human freedom. That is to say, in affirming that human goodness is a possibility, one is affirming that human beings are free. Whether this affirmation is an empirical claim or has some other status is an issue which exercised Kant.

(b) In denying that human goodness is a possibility, one may be linking an empirical claim that no human being has exemplified human goodness, to a claim that in all probability no human being will do so. This view involves some empirical beliefs, about what the past is like, plus some empirical beliefs about human nature and its potential for change. It does also, however, involve beliefs about the nature of goodness, and about what it would be like for human beings to embody or exemplify goodness, and therefore about what it would be for us to recognize such goodness. Now such beliefs about goodness are not straightforward, empirical beliefs. The consequence of this is that the denial that no human being has or will embody good is a view which, although it cannot be adequately stated without embodying *some* empirical beliefs, certainly is not entailed by those empirical beliefs, and in most cases would not entail those *specific* beliefs.

For example, one might deny that the Desert Fathers embody goodness either because one is claiming that our picture of them is based upon historical error, or because their reputation for goodness is based upon what Hume disparagingly referred to as 'the whole train of monkish virtues', which are 'not real virtue at all'. And so one might argue, in the case of *any* proposed exemplification of goodness. Either affirmation or denial requires both empirical and conceptual constituents.

(c) Finally, one might as a pessimist allow that there have been, and there may continue to be, unambiguously good deeds and people, but argue that this is such a rare phenomenon that either we may discount them, or even we may talk of the goodness being lost or overwhelmed by evil. This form of pessimism rests upon at least one of two different beliefs. Either it is assumed that the significance of one good deed, or one good man, can be lost; or it is assumed that goodness is not in the end particular – not, that is to say, the goodness of *this* act, or *this* woman, but something either abstract or composite. In this latter case one can acknowledge the goodness of deed or person, but regard this as insufficient ground for rejecting pessimism. As we consider talk of the possibility of goodness understood as a claim about intelligibility, we shall explore the implications of this further.

(2) 'The difference between optimism and pessimism is a difference about the intelligibility of the claim that goodness is a human possibility.' On this account we are dealing with a very radical form of pessimism indeed. What is at stake is whether the claim that Socrates or Jesus of Nazareth was a good man has any meaning at all. In this the radical pessimist differs from the cynic, for one may well be cynical about the legitimacy of regarding any individual as good, without necessarily questioning the intelligibility of the suggestion.

The heart of the view which I am offering is that the 'work' of Jesus is the establishment of the possibility of optimism. His achievement is that he has given intelligible form to the claim that human goodness is a possibility.

To argue that human goodness is a possiblity is to argue that particular human goodness is a possibility. A weaker interpretation of this is the fairly trivial claim that if human goodness is a possibility, then it follows that it is possible for at least one human being to exhibit goodness. The stronger version, however, to which I adhere, is that the essential form of goodness is particular. By this I mean that unless we can envisage what it would be like for a particular human being to embody goodness, then we have not established that human goodness is a possibility. (Conversely, I should also affirm that if we can envisage or show what it would be like for a particular human being to embody goodness, then we have shown that goodness is a human possibility, and we have gone as far as we can towards establishing the intelligibility of this idea.)

This point having been made we can now pause briefly to take our bearings and to erect a couple of theological signposts.

I have been trying to clarify one of many possible versions of optimism, and in so doing I have, I believe, identified the most radical form of pessimism – that which denies the reality of the distinction between good and evil. To espouse this form of optimism, it has been argued, is to affirm something about human beings – that it is conceivable that they might recognize in their lives the distinction between good and evil. If this is true, it will be an essential element of any doctrine of man, with wide implications for theology. The second point which has been uncovered, and to consideration of which I now turn, is that this form of optimism involves affirming at least one element of belief in the incarnation, namely that it is conceivable that goodness might incarnate itself in particular form.

In my account of optimism so far, I have been concentrating attention upon the argument from possibility, understood as intelligibility, to reality. However, in the case of the incarnation it might well seem as if the position is reversed: surely, it might be claimed, the situation in which

the Christian theologian finds himself is much more straightforward. Can he not argue that in Jesus we have at least one
case of human goodness, and that therefore we can argue that
ipso facto the possibility of human goodness has been established. The argument would run as follows:

(1) Jesus of Nazareth incarnates, or particularizes in
    human form, goodness;
(2) human goodness is thus realized in history;
(3) this is the justification for optimism, for the belief that
    human goodness is a possibility.

If this argument worked it would certainly resolve many of
the difficulties surrounding the discussion of optimism and
pessimism. However, as it stands, it both distorts a number
of important elements in the situation, and also fails to confront a number of problems.

In the first place there remain all those exegetical problems
uncovered in chapter 9, of precisely what picture of the
historical Jesus is available to us. Both the so-called 'old' and
'new' quests for the historical Jesus run into the uncertainties
of historical scholarship. The difficulties which historians of
the New Testament have in finding an undisputed basis for
indicating what form particularized or incarnated goodness
actually took, are fundamental difficulties for any such argument as the one under consideration. As I have already conceded, my own account may be vulnerable on this score, but
I shall argue that this lends weight to rather than defeats my
central contention.

The second problem which faces the argument from the
historical Jesus directly to the belief that human goodness is a
possibility, was elaborated in detail in chapter 10. There is a
whole host of difficulties to be encountered in the process of
trying to give an account of what it means to say that perfect
goodness can be given particular form. If I am correct in my
argument that it was not a failure of technique which denied
Dostoevsky his literary goal of 'the representation of a truly
perfect and noble man', then inevitably we must find the
problem in the nature of goodness itself. This is the view

which we found in Kierkegaard in his refusal to give a description of the good man in terms which would tolerate the idea of the unambiguous portrayal of goodness in external or objective form. These points are of telling significance for any attempt to base a Christology, or an argument about the basis for optimism, on even a *relatively* detailed picture of Jesus.

For both these reasons I cannot accept the argument as it stands, from the historical figure to the possibility of human goodness.

One response to the analysis which I have been developing would be to argue that it is unacceptably idealist in emphasis. It could seem as if in the end I am wholeheartedly endorsing the arguments of those who argue that whether Jesus lived or not is of no ultimate significance. Certainly I have been arguing that the possibility or intelligibility of what it is believed that he manifests – goodness incarnate in particular form – is the essential basis for the rejection of radical pessimism. As such, it might seem, Myshkin, had Dostoevsky succeeded, or Melville's Billy Budd, or indeed any other appropriate fictional character, will do. Indeed, one of the things which certain forms of literature do *par excellence* is to establish possibilities. Why then bother with the tiresome problems of the historical Jesus, rather than with the much simpler issue of the story, which might or might not be true, but which can quite adequately define the possibility of human goodness? This view parallels Harvey's admission that, 'The conclusion one is driven to is that the content of faith can as well be mediated through a historically false story *of a certain kind* as through a true one, through a myth as well as through history';[4] or, we might add, through a novel, as through a gospel.

This puts the issue in a form which is both aggressive and clear, but the clarity is deceptive, and, as I hope to show, it will result in a failure to appreciate some crucial aspects of the concept of goodness operating in the life and teaching of Jesus.

To revert to an earlier point, the importance of the historical figure is based upon the idea of the work of Jesus. The historical figure is important because what that man achieved was the embodiment, the manifestation, the incarnation of goodness, but in a manner that is appropriate to the nature of such goodness and therefore, because this is the only way possible, indirectly communicates to us what that goodness is. In this we are following the lead given by Kierkegaard rather than Dostoevsky. In so doing we are conceding that Dostoevsky could not ever have succeeded in the 'miracle' of 'the manifestation of the beautiful', or 'the representation of a truly perfect and noble man', or if he did succeed it would be through a deliberate failure. This of course sounds at best paradoxical, at worst silly. The point at issue revolves round the question of what manner of manifestation is appropriate to the nature of the goodness in question.

Before we ask, 'Does the figure of Jesus incarnate or manifest perfect goodness?', we must first ask, 'If perfect goodness has been incarnated or particularized, what would we expect to be true of the individual in question?' First and foremost, what would have to be true is that the individual in question, by the pattern of word and deed, does not mislead us as to the nature of that goodness, for example into thinking that it can be directly communicated or described in such a way that it can be unambiguously 'read off' from the life and words in question.

My argument will be that in this historical figure these conditions are met. In him we find a twofold movement at work which brings out very well the importance of indirectness here. Awareness of this duality is dependent upon an appreciation of how this historical figure transforms our notion of what the manifestation of goodness is. The duality in question is that the figure of Jesus of Nazareth at one and the same time both demands to be recognized as the incarnation of goodness in particular form, and also denies that it is possible to affirm confidently that he is such. (It should be noted that in my use of 'demands' and 'denies' here, I am not forgetting all the difficulties of historical scepticism raised earlier. The legitimation of the use of these terms is to be found in the response of disciples in both first and twentieth centuries.)

By way of clarification it is necessary to distinguish this case from the cases of both Socrates and the Buddha. Socrates played the part of the teacher and the midwife who all the while realized and taught that as such he was dispensable. At best he was the occasion for learning on the part of the pupil. In a comparable way the Buddha rejects the interest which his disciples show in him, and directs them instead to the way of enlightenment which he teaches. The way in which the figure of Jesus denies to his followers the legitimacy of confidently affirming that he is goodness incarnate in particular form, is quite different form either of these cases.

In the first place, on the only occasion on which he might be thought explicitly to deny to others the right to affirm that he is good, we are not obviously dealing with a comparable situation, for it is to the rich young man who does *not* accept his advice to whom he says, 'Why callest thou me good? There is none good but one, that is God.' It is the nature of both the goodness which he defines, and the way in which he manifests it, rather than explicit teaching comparable to that of the Buddha or Socrates, which prevents any straightforward move from 'He is good' to 'Goodness is a possibility.' Thus although one can say of both the Buddha and Socrates, in one sense, that it would not matter if they were not historical figures, the situation is not exactly comparable with the case of Jesus.

The central reason for this is to be found in the question which this historical figure provokes. This shows itself in a number of ways, of which the most direct is the questions which we are forced to ask by the very suggestion made by the historicity of this man, that the form of goodness is particular rather than general and that it is to be found embodied in a human being. Surely we are forced to ask what such a human being looks like? How is goodness manifest? What are the individuating descriptions which help us identify *this* man as good? The answer given to these questions in, for example, the closing chapters of the fourth gospel contains the essential elements of this double movement to which I have referred. Thus whereas the discourses of chapters 14 to 16 instruct the disciples constantly to see God in him, to see him as 'the way', as the one who seeks the obedience of those who obey his commands, they lead to the address to God in chapter 17: 'Father, the hour is come. Glorify thy Son, that the Son may glorify thee.' This leads to vilification, ridicule, crucifixion and the words *on the cross*, 'It is finished!' The picture is at once the insistence that 'I am in the Father, and the Father in me', and also the apparent denial of this by his very fate.

The point is this: one particular human being both affirms that he is 'the way', and at the same time apparently deliberately divests himself of every outer sign of divinity by the fate which he accepts. My argument is that *one* element of this 'kenosis' is that it forces the theological kenosis which prevents the theologian from unequivocally and unambiguously asserting,

(1) Jesus of Nazareth incarnates, or particularizes in human form, goodness.

Ipso facto this historical figure (if the implicit interpretation can be defended) prevents us, by the very conception of goodness at issue, from claiming unequivocally and unambiguously

(2) Human goodness is thus realized in history.

A fortiori we cannot then conclude,

(3) This is the justification for optimism, for the belief that human goodness is a possibility.

The point is that the conception of goodness which is made manifest in human form is a conception of goodness which does not contain any external sign of vindication of that goodness, for such an external sign would be incompatible with the idea of crucifixion. It is for this reason, I believe, that we find emphasized in Bonhoeffer's lectures on Christology the ambiguity and hiddenness implicit in the notion of incarnation.

'Ambiguity' and 'hiddenness' are *one* way of trying to conceptualize a point. A rather different way would be to tell a mythic story. Suppose God were to want to teach human beings this truth about the essential inwardness of goodness, how best might he do so? First, perhaps, he might teach them to think about the very idea that such goodness might be particularized in human form, and do so by offering a historical figure who might seem to present or at least be taken to present the possibility of describing or defining, by how he lived, the outward form of goodness. However, being God he is aware of two things (amongst others!): the first is that an historical figure becomes progressively unavailable to succeeding generations, and that as these later ages become sophisticated about the nature of historical research, they will become increasingly sceptical about whether the picture of this man which they have inherited can bear the burden of revealing such an important truth; the second point is that God is equally well aware that if the outward form of this historical life is to communicate what is essential about such goodness, it must do so by pointing away from itself to the inner life.

Fortunately these two points can be made to cohere with one another. The importance of the historical is in this sense not diminished by the problems of finding an agreed picture of the historical Jesus. The difficulty of doing this is no more than we should expect of an historical manifestation or incarnation of perfect goodness. It would constitute a problem only if one were committed to arguing from the premiss that Jesus manifested in outward *form* the nature of perfect goodness. His life and words, particularly as the latter foreshadowed the manner of his death, point clearly to the inadequacy of any account of goodness which is essentially outward and unambiguous.

This is a lesson which, in a related context, was stressed by Kierkegaard in his discussion of indirect communication.

Certainly goodness must have particular form if it is to be a human possibility. But the figure of Jesus of Nazareth, as we find it portrayed in the fourth gospel, both claims that this is so, states in no uncertain terms 'Ecce Homo', *and in that very assertion* teaches us the truth of Kierkegaard's insistence that the good man 'is incognito, but his incognito consists in having an appearance entirely like others'. Thus, if we say that the possibility of human goodness is established by the figure of Jesus, we are not arguing in any straightforward way from particular to general, the point being, that we are never in a position to unequivocally assert (1). The realization that this is so, however, arises from meditation upon the implications of being confronted by this particular historical figure who, in what I have called a 'two-fold movement', both seems to give and take away the basis of optimism – the possibility of goodness in particular form.

This brief outline should, I hope, at least moderate the charge of idealism. I am *not* arguing that the historical figure is unimportant, or is merely an example of a universal truth. Rather I am arguing that the account offered of what is being taught about the nature of goodness, by this historical figure, is such that a straightforward deduction from

(1a) this is a good man,

to

(3a) human goodness is a possibility,

involves multiple errors. It distorts the nature of goodness by making it appear as if it were a quality which can be individuated, described, and judged unambiguously to be present or absent. It distorts what the idea of crucifixion reveals about the nature of Jesus' goodness. Consequently it distorts what basis, if any, optimism has. Finally, it distorts the relationship between historicity and faith.

The conclusions which I draw from this exploration can be stated fairly concisely. The optimist is the man who believes that goodness is a human possibility. He argues that this is so because he believes that the distinction between goodness and evil is intelligible and as such is a *real* distinction. That this is so is manifest in, but not established by, 'the life, sayings, deeds and death' of Jesus of Nazareth. The nature of its manifestation is such that it could not be *established* by the historical or particular individual. The historical figure provokes us to ask what the particular good man looks like, and, in a sense, the answer is 'not like anything in particular', although the particular form of his life does actually reveal this.

The optimist affirms a reality by affirming a possibility. In this very austere form of optimism, the affirmation does not depend upon an individual example, for it cannot. Neither single nor multiple cases can establish this, for, again in the words of Kierkegaard, the 'individual' (goodness in particular form) 'is a stranger in the world of the finite, but does not manifest his heterogeneity, his separation from worldliness by a foreign mode of dress. This would be a contradiction, since he would thereby qualify himself in a worldly manner.'[5] The optimist affirms the reality of such a mode of goodness, and at the same time gives it content, and although I shall state rather than develop this point, one aspect of the content thus given to the notion of goodness is important. The idea of goodness which does emerge from the crucifixion is central to the idea of the triumph of the good. If the word 'triumph' is relevant here, it is so for this reason: in the words, 'I pray not that thou shouldest take them out of the world, but that thou shouldest keep them from evil,' the writer of the fourth gospel is foreshadowing the crucifixion that is to come. The optimist who is a Christian believer affirms his optimism by insisting that Jesus was delivered up completely to the world, but was not overcome by evil. Alongside this prayer, that is a peculiarly powerful way of affirming a truth about what is a *human* possibility. Conversely, however, seeing the prayer in the light of what is to happen to the man who uttered the prayer, is to deny to even the Christian optimist an objective and unambiguous case which will *establish* his position over against the radical pessimist.[6]

Part IV

Conclusion

13

The Legacy of Theism

The title of this chapter indicates quite clearly the proposal which this book makes. It is arguable that the most significant constitutive element of European culture is Christian theism. Any adequate understanding of that culture must come to an assessment of that legacy. The assessment, however, must not confine itself to the descriptive, for one's intellectual and spiritual heritage is a way of seeing and living which one inhabits, and which is either in the process of decay or in the process of revision. Thus an adequate assessment must recognize that one is harnessed to what is in continuing process of change. Further, it must engage with the processes of change as one's best judgement proposes. This book has been an attempt to do just that.

It would be impossible to disentangle all the elements of our culture which are a consequence of Christianity: history does not work in such a pedantic fashion. However, recognition that Christianity is part of our history, and as such has a history of its own, has been perhaps the most significant single stimulus to theological reflection in the last one hundred and fifty years. Believers have reacted in many ways to this, but there tend to be two broad emphases which emerge. On the one hand there are those who emphasize the continuity of the tradition running back for almost two thousand years. The danger here is to underestimate the richness of the tradition and the theological significance of historicity from the earliest days. On the other hand there are those who would emphasize the radical changes which have taken place within the growth of Christianity, and who would as a consequence fall prey to the dangers of severing connections altogether.

Doubtless some will see my conclusions as too radical on the idea of God and others will find me too conservative on the figure of Jesus. These, however, are specific criticisms of my conclusions, and before discussing them I wish to underline a more general point about the nature of the enquiry. Whether or not what I have written about the concept of God or the figure of Jesus is mistaken is a matter of judgement based on argument: what is not equally open to argument is the legitimacy of the endeavour. The resources of our culture are too precious to be squandered in a facile rejection of religion, or in intellectually feeble or spiritually small-minded protectionism. If the legacy of Christian theism is to be more than the responsibility to dispose of the cadaver as decently as possible, then exercises such as the present one will be the outward sign of it. That some will fall into error is almost inevitable, but if even the questions are right, that will be a sign of life and of health rather than decline.

The questions which I have set must be asked by each generation, for they are the necessary correctives to slovenly thought and superstitious belief. My own proposals for answering them are represented in the three main parts of the book. It is certainly the case that the negative conclusions of the first part have positive outcome in the second and third parts, but equally there is some loss. Positively the agnosticism of these early chapters allows a re-examination of the central intellectual content of Christian theism, *viz.* the intelligibility of the idea of a view of human affairs *sub specie aeternitatis*. The importance of this idea cannot be underestimated, and the capacity to envisage such a possibility is arguably definitive of human nature and of the human condition. A claim which bears both reflection and reiteration is Kierkegaard's proposal that, 'a genuine human being as a synthesis of the finite and the infinite finds his reality in holding these two factors together'.[1] Theism has been both the expression and the protection of this perspective and of the form of life in which it is embodied. Thus although I do believe that this is the central *intellectual* legacy of Christian theism, this should not be taken as an invitation to dismiss my proposals as 'intellectualism' or the like: such a reaction is ignorant of the power of ideas to shape the way we live and feel. Surely religion above all demonstrates the truth of this.

However, positive as such an outcome is, there is much in this opening section which must appear devastatingly negative. The idea of God as an individual has gone, and with it must surely go the power and weight of the anthropomorphism of the imaginings and sayings of the theism of communal and individual piety. For some, such a loss will be too great to contemplate, but before all my proposals are consequently set aside I must make three points. The first is psychologically and socially important, but of less intellectual weight than the other two. None the less, in the present context it is important to remind ourselves that for many the anthropomorphic images of God and the liturgy which depends upon them are dead. This is doubtless so for a variety of reasons. At one level it is worth reflecting both that the worst excesses of religion often go hand in hand with the most anthropomorphic accounts of God, and that this is probably due to the fact that the most deeply anthropomorphic images of God are the most tribal, and consequently the least emancipated from monotheism's origins in polytheism. At another level, there are important elements within the Christian tradition which have consistently throughout the centuries struggled to divest themselves of the trappings of religious belief understood as a relationship to a being or person called 'God'.

The second point which I must make is to call attention once again to the argument of chapter 2. A theology which starts from the realities of suffering and evil in the world cannot avoid a high degree of agnosticism in its affirmations about God: the alternative is to start from a conception of God which is at least personal, and then, as was shown, to end up in the subterfuges of an unsatisfactory and selective appeal to 'mystery', as an attempt to bypass the problem of evil. The only alternative to this is to jettison moral criteria as irrelevant to the formation of religious belief. The dangers of such a procedure, whether explicit or implicit, are so obvious as to require no further statement. Those who would push aside the agnosticism of Part One may only legitimately do so if they answer the points made there. This is not a demand to 'solve' the so-called problem of evil: initially it is a request for good reason to concur in the practice of assuming relative clarity and certainty about the metaphysical attributes of God, while engulfing his moral attributes in a fog of mystery and incomprehensibility. The inconsistency here is religiously dangerous as well as philosophically unacceptable.

The third point to be made is again one of challenge. At the heart of traditional theism is the belief in a personal God who acts in history and in the world. It is important to spell out the belief in this way, for essentially the theistic base from which my agnostic conclusions may be attacked must be at least this. The challenge which I would make is outlined in chapter 4, for it is the request to give *some* account of how such a God is related to the world. If we are to talk of a God who acts, we must be speaking of a relationship between such a God and particular tracts of space and time – particular places where he acts, and particular times when such acts take place. Of course this is a crude way of putting the issue, but that is just the point, for I believe that the idea of such an act or deed is incompatible with the idea of an eternal God. Acts and deeds are particular: they have spatio-temporal locations. The one exception to this, for which a good case can be made, is a mental act, where the insistence on spatial location is disputable to the extent that it *may* only be a contingent fact that mental acts seem in the case of human beings to have a spatial location. The outcome of this argument will depend upon one's view of the conceivability of disembodied existence,[2] but even so temporal co-ordinates will be required for the deed in question. Further, none of the traditional accounts of God seem to be satisfied with the idea of a God who is confined in his acts to thinking, imagining, wishing, etc., for traditional belief seems to require a God who might change the world. Thus the price of the rejection of the agnostic conclusions of the opening chapters is high, and it does not seem to me that traditional theism has sufficient intellectual capital to pay it.

I do not accept, however, that the consequence is that we must totally reject the rich inheritance of theism, for as I have argued in the second section of the book, what lies at the very heart of theism does not depend upon the idea of a God who is an individual, and – to the extent that he is conceived of in personal terms – anthropomorphic. What theism has pre-served is the possibility of a view of human affairs which is not reducible to the view of an individual or group of indi-viduals.

The answer which I offer to the question raised *via* Hep-burn in the opening chapter, of what would be lost 'if we were to abandon all talk of God', can now be given: we would lose the idea of the vision of human affairs *sub specie aeternitatis*. I find it difficult to imagine anything which would have more far-reaching consequences. It might be argued that such a perspective can be found elsewhere than in the preservation of the language of theism. If that is so I should like to see the case made out. In part II I have pre-sented my own arguments to show first that the idea of a view of human affairs *sub specie aeternitatis* is intelligible; second, what the content of such an idea both is and is not; and third, how such an idea is and has been intimately con-nected with Christian theism.

The exemplification of this idea is – for all the arguments offered in chapter 10 – impossibly difficult. If the proposed exemplification is the figure of Jesus, then as I have indicated in chapter 9, there are all the additional problems associated with finding the exemplification in a historical figure. Since the difficulties of this for Christian theism cannot be avoided, I found it necessary to indicate my own approach to the questions of the relation between history and faith in chapters

9 and 11. However, this was not simply an academic detour, for it laid the ground for my account of the appropriateness of the dialectic of the closing chapters of the fourth gospel, where it is both affirmed that Jesus is the Christ, and denied by the fate which befalls him that he is the Christ whom men expected and awaited. This pattern of affirmation and denial is, for the reasons given in the argument, the only way in which one can do justice to the peculiar nature of the claim that human beings can, and indeed must, find intelligible the possibility of a view of human affairs *sub specie aeternitatis*.

Thus I am making claims not simply for the importance of the inheritance of theism in general, but for the importance of Christian theism in particular. For it is at the heart of Christian theism in the centuries of Christological debate that we find the most sustained western engagement within the issues which arise when once we posit the possibility of the intersection of the eternal and the temporal, the finite and the infinite, in the lives of human beings. That this is so becomes clearer if we cease to define theism in terms of a belief in a supernatural person called 'God'. Indeed for all the much-protested radicalness of books such as *The Myth of God Incarnate*,[3] my own dissatisfaction with that book and the debate which followed arises from the fact that for the most part the argument takes place in the context of the ground rules laid down by traditional theism – ground rules rejected here in the light of the argument of chapters 2 and 4.

The inheritance of Christian theism is thus defined as having two related aspects: in the first place it is the statement of the belief that it is possible to see this world and our place in it *sub specie aeternitatis*. We must remind ourselves, however, that 'possibility' here is not simply 'empirical possibility': what is simply empirically possible may or may not be found in the world and therefore is only possibly real. The possibility of which I have written in this book is rather a claim about the way the world is: either the world is such that it is possible to conceive of it *sub specie aeternitatis* or it is not. In either case one is saying something about the way things are. The optimism of my view is that the world is such that the radical pessimism which rejects goodness as a human possibility is mistaken, for that rejection is the rejection of the distinction between what is good and what is evil. Whether there is such a distinction is a matter of ontology, but one in the end of whether the structures of reality are such that the distinction is *intelligible*.

The second aspect of the inheritance of Christian theism is closely related but distinct from this. If, as I have argued, the world is such that we may see human affairs *sub specie aeternitatis*, then we must confront the question of the manner of the intersection of the temporal and the eternal in human affairs. If, again as I have argued, the eternal is not to be encountered as an element or aspect of the temporal, then this poses peculiar problems. Essentially this is the problem at the heart of *Christian* theism. It shows itself in a variety of ways, for example in the doctrine of the incarnation, of the divinity or otherwise of Jesus. How can what is eternal manifest itself in the temporal? How can what is perfect have particular form? Minimally the Christian tradition gives us as our inheritance the most sophisticated treatment of these questions which European civilization affords. However, in the final chapters of the book I have argued for a much stronger conclusion than that, for I have claimed that in the more subtle treatments of the figure of Jesus there is offered an approach to these matters which is both distinctive and definitive.

If such is the inheritance of Christian theism from which I have tried to construct a system of belief, how is such a construction of revision to be evaluated? On the scale of orthodoxy it would not rate very highly: its score as a descriptive account of what Christian theists do believe, or have believed, would be equally low. In the first chapter I did suggest some criteria which might be used to evaluate any such enterprise, and I propose to conclude the book by a brief consideration of how far my proposed revisionary theology satisfies them.

The first criterion states that any successful revision of the content of religious belief must be undertaken in the context of European culture as a whole. This is the statement of a requirement of the intellectual and spiritual context in which theological reflection must be carried out if theology is not to lose contact with the heights of the culture in which we live. I have tried at various points to show where at least some of the points of connection are to be found. However, at best my argument has taken some limited steps towards meeting the demands of this criterion. In mitigation I can plead the necessity of starting where the various elements of the argument are to be found, and in so far as I must take as one starting point where theology is mostly to be found, it has meant a fairly limited engagement with the intersections between very specific questions arising out of the Christian tradition and the broader correlated enquiries to be found elsewhere. None the less, it is legitimate to claim that something more than gestures have been made here, and that the discussions of the manner of Dostoevsky's treatment of the problems of the particularization of perfect goodness (chapter 9), and of some approaches to the problems of evil and suffering (chapter 3) bear this out. Equally important is the fact that implicitly my arguments have, I hope, consistently been alert to the problems posed for theology respectively by two dominant intellectual legacies: the first is the philosophy of Immanuel Kant; and the second is the growth in European sensibility since the seventeenth century of awareness of the fact that religion as well as other dimensions of human life has a history.

The second criterion gave a central place to moral considerations in the construction of a theology: a religious belief which runs countr to our moral beliefs is to that extent unacceptable. I feel on rather firmer ground here, for this thought has dominated all that has been written. Of course, there are problems about the connotations of this, and some of these had to be dealt with at some length. However, the second chapter clearly set the tone of all that was to come by making the so-called moral attributes central to the conception of God. The implications of this for the priority or otherwise of the moral over the religious is, predictably, a little more complex than might appear at first sight and some of the implications of this were discussed in more detail in chapter 3. The further related point on which quite certainly more work is required is the question of the insights of the saint. If these include moral innovations, as they well might, then we must find some way of assuring ourselves in accord with this criterion that we are talking of moral insights and not pathological ramblings. Chapter 7 gives some indication of how I should want to begin to approach this problem.

The third criterion concerns the comprehensiveness of the system: the acceptability of a form of religious belief is related to its comprehensiveness in the sense which it makes of our experience of the world in which we find ourselves. I should want to argue that I have met the demands of this criterion up to a point. In the first place I have met the spirit of the demand by trying to show the immense adaptability of Christian theism. Even those who would disagree with the need for the specific adaptions which I have proposed may, none the less, agree upon the importance of showing that the Christian tradition has the depth and intellectual richness necessary to adapt to and accommodate new intellectual insights.

There is a different dimension to comprehensiveness which I have tried to take account of in two related ways. In the very attempt to found a system of belief and a way of life upon the idea of a vision of the world *sub specie aeternitatis*, I have given the firmest possible underlining to the idea that a system of belief must, like Sir Thomas More, be 'for all seasons'. In a related discussion I have made overtures to the point that a revisionary theology must be defined in terms of what might possibly be or come to be the case, rather than simply limit itself to responses to what actually is the case. Whereas attempts to interpret the figure of Jesus by discounting his historicity may leave us uncertain about how to decide whether a particular response of the tradition to change within our society is legitimate or illegitimate, an overemphasis upon a particular account of his history may prove dangerously limiting because by becoming too detailed, too particular, it excludes finally the responsiveness and flexibility to change which has been till now the strength which has kept Christianity alive. In the account which I have given of the historicity of Jesus – historicity *per se* combined with a due respect for the ambiguities and hiddenness which are inevitable on my account of the relation between the temporal and the eternal – I believe that the comprehensivess of the possibilities to which the tradition can respond has been retained. It is important to stress again that this is not the consequence of an *ad hoc* reassessment of the historicity of Jesus in the wake of a rather eccentric philosophical view. It is rather that this treatment of the question of the historical Jesus is the development of elements already within the tradition. These elements are not *the* tradition – whatever that might mean – but the ambiguity of the figure of Jesus, the uncertainty about how to assess or interpret the details of his teaching, or the 'facts' of his life, are as old as the tradition itself. There is a sense in which the question 'Who do you say that I am?' cannot be definitively answered; for all the logical questions which we encountered about the particularization of the eternal have parallels in any attempt to find the words to answer that question.

There is one sense of 'comprehensiveness' to which I have certainly not sufficiently addressed myself. Clearly if a system of beliefs is to be comprehensive in its scope, then it must show its capacity to respond to a very wide range of situations and contexts. A believer, one who inhabits that system of belief, must not, in principle, find himself at a loss. If the belief system is comprehensive in that sense, then, again in principle, there should not be situations which arise which fall completely outside the system and thus show its limitations. The great religions which have survived for centuries show their strength in precisely this way, and doing so is a condition of their survival. This is a point which is separate from the question of their truth, but is almost equally important if one is talking of a system of beliefs rather than simply individual beliefs.

The difficulty for this essay is, of course, that there is no way of finally testing the comprehensiveness of a system, for one cannot envisage 'all possible situations'. Ultimately only time will tell whether a system is even relatively-speaking comprehensive. But what must be admitted is that there are implications here for my proposed system of belief which will require at least a further volume to follow them through in satisfactory fashion. For example, there are two important areas which any system of belief must address in a way that will fashion and structure responses to the questions which they raise: the relation between religious belief and matters of social and political concern, and the view to be adopted of the plurality of religions in our world. How does the world of social planning and political strategy look *sub specie aeternitatis*? The questions here will test very deeply the extent to which the system proposed is too individualistic, or simply pie in the eternal sky. For that very reason they require profounder and fuller treatment than one could hope for as part of a book whose focus must necessarily lie elsewhere. Likewise the problems faced by any religious view when set in the context of religious pluralism are very far-reaching indeed. In fact Christianity and Islam, for example, have hardly begun to grapple with these and it may prove to be their undoing. In this book I have decided to avoid the demands of fashion and have refused to make *gestures* towards the discussion of religious pluralism. Consequently I have deliberately worked within the traditions of Christianity and European culture more broadly conceived. This is not because I believe the problems of the plurality of religions to be unimportant. Quite the reverse. They cannot be dealt with in the odd paragraph, or even chapter here and there. What I do accept is that unless the system of belief outlined in this book can furnish us with a more adequate approach to these matters than traditional Christian theism has done, it will be so much the less comprehensive, and so much the poorer. Further, if a view such as the one which I have outlined cannot equip us conceptually to formulate adequate ways of approaching questions of religion and politics or the plurality of religions, it will fail to measure up to the demands made of it by this third criterion.

The fourth criterion is equally difficult to respond to in any final way: a revisionary account of religious belief both commends itself and avoids the dangers of reductionism to the extent to which it gives or preserves insights which are not available elsewhere – into the human condition, or into the world in which we live. The main element of my reply to the question implicit in this must be to point to my central positive conclusions in the second part of the book. My argument there was that the central inheritance of theism is the idea of the possibility of a view of human affairs *sub specie aeternitatis*. If my claim that such a view is intelligible and is shown to be such in the exposition of this revisionary theology, then I have gone a long way towards meeting this criterion, for if my 'theology' can encapsulate this possibility then it certainly does avoid the danger of a reductionist slide into naturalism. It also offers an insight into both the affairs of men and the way the world is, which is not readily available outside of theistic views. There will be those who may contend that it is possible to show the intelligibility of such a view without resting upon religious foundations. If so, the onus is upon them to show that this is possible.

In summary, my proposal is that theism has preserved in a unique and living fashion the possibility of a view of our world *sub specie aeternitatis*. This inheritance, as expounded, is anti-relativistic, and is possible only in a context where the idea of transcendence is given central place. Equally important, however, is the knowledge that the questions of the intersection between the finite and the infinite, the eternal and the temporal, are given due recognition and treated with the appropriate subtlety. Pre-eminently is this true of the careful and sophisticated treatment of the figure of Jesus, which is both the crown of the Christian tradition and the hallmark of good theology. The figure of Jesus as presented in strands of the Christian tradition provokes in a definitive way the question of the nature of the eternal and its manifestation in the world of space and time. Equally the inheritance of theism includes the cultivation of an awareness of the importance of the eternal in human life, and of the habits of thought and reflection which accompany that.

The final criterion, that of truth, is perhaps the most difficult to apply: a revisionary account of religious belief is
acceptable to the extent to which it makes and defends a
claim to be true. The first element of this is clear and comparatively easy to respond to, and yet it is exceptionally important. Its importance lies in the fact that it excludes any
attempts to analyse religious beliefs as a series of attitudes to,
rather than beliefs about, reality. Thus I accept the need to see
the centrality of the belief that the world can be viewed *sub
specie aeternitatis*, as a claim *about the world* and not a claim
about the *attitudes* which men and women may adopt *to the
world*. In the terms of this criterion I am *making* this claim. In
the course of this book I have also defended it. Whether my
defence constitutes a sufficient basis for it to be accepted as
true is perhaps more arguable. Indeed, as I have already
accepted in my comments on the third and fourth criteria,
further discussion and elaboration is necessary. My revisionary theology stands or falls not simply by what is argued
within this book, but also by the further explorations which
the arguments here entail.

The way in which the claims of such a revisionary
theology might be shown to be true are complex, but that is
equally true of traditional beliefs. In neither case is that good
reason for ceasing to try to uncover what is true of our
world, and whether it is more or less truly seen if it is seen *sub
specie aeternitatis*.

Notes

Chapter 1 The Changing Face of Belief

1 John Locke, *Essay Concerning Human Understanding* III, X. 23.
2 P. Geach, *God and the Soul*, Routledge, 1969, p. 74.
3 The *Scotsman*, 20 May 1981.
4 R. W. Hepburn, *Christianity and Paradox*, Watts, 1958, p. 21.
5 Iris Murdoch, *The Sovereignty of Good*, Routledge, 1970.
6 Stuart Hampshire, *Thought and Action*, Chatto and Windus, 1959, pp. 206–7.

Chapter 2 God and Evil: Starting All Over Again

1 Plato, *Republic* 380b.
2 Plato, *Timaeus* 30a.
3 Ibid., 47e.
4 See J. L. Mackie, 'Evil and Omnipotence', *Mind*, 1955, reprinted in *The Philosophy of Religion*, B. Mitchell (ed.), Oxford University Press, 1971; B. Mitchell, *The Justification of Religious Belief*, Macmillan, 1973, pp. 9–10; R. F. Holland, *Against Empiricism*, Basil Blackwell, 1980, ch. 15.
5 John Le Carré, *Smiley's People*, Hodder and Stoughton, 1979, pp. 307–8.
6 R. Swinburne, *The Existence of God*, Oxford University Press, 1981, p. 273.
7 *The Justification of Religious Belief*, p. 44.
8 J. Hick, *Evil and the God of Love*, Macmillan, 1966, pp. 371–2.
9 H. Kung, *On Being a Christian*, Collins, 1978, p. 431.

10   H. Kung, *Does God Exist*, Collins, 1980, p. 674.
11   *Against Empiricism*, ch. 7.

Chapter 3   *Religious Belief and Moral Commitment*

1   Plato, *Euthyphro* 10a.
2   F. Waismann, 'Verifiability', *Proc. Aris. Soc.* supp. XIX, reprinted in A. Flew (ed.), *Logic and Language* I, Basil Blackwell, 1951.
3   A. MacIntyre and P. Ricoeur, *The Religious Significance of Atheism*, Columbia University Press, 1969, p. 32.
4   John Wisdom, *Paradox and Discovery*, Basil Blackwell, 1965, p. 146.
5   H. L. Hart, *The Concept of Law*, Oxford University Press, 1961, p. 125.

Chapter 4   *God, Eternity and Agnosticism*

1   Nelson Pike, *God and Timelessness*, Routledge, 1970.
2   Richard Swinburne, *The Coherence of Theism*, Oxford University Press, 1977.
3   A. N. Prior, 'The Formalities of Omniscience', *Philosophy*, 1962, reprinted in *Papers on Time and Tense*, Oxford University Press.
4   P. Helm, 'Timelessness and Foreknowledge', *Mind*, 1975, p. 524.
5   See David Hume, *Dialogues Concerning Natural Religion*, part V.
6   M. F. Wiles, *Faith and the Mystery of God*, SCM Press, 1982, p. 13.
7   A number of the central arguments of this chapter were first presented to the Aristotelian Society in 'God, Time and Eternity' (*Proc. Aris. Soc.* 1978–9).

Chapter 5   *Theology: the Articulation of the Possible*

1   *Summa Theologiae* la, 1, 7, from the 'Blackfriars' edition, vol. I, trans. O.P. Thomas Gilby, Eyre and Spottiswoode, 1964.

2   Karl Barth, *Church Dogmatics* I, *The Doctrine of the Word of God*,
    T. & T. Clark, 1963, 1.II.1.81.
3   Don Cupitt, *Taking Leave of God*, and *The World to Come*,
    SCM Press, 1980 and 1982.
4   Paul Tillich, *Systematic Theology* I, James Nisbet, 1953, p. 263.
5   I. Kant, *Critique of Pure Reason*, trans. N. Kemp Smith, Mac-
    millan, 1961, preface to the second edition, p. 29.
6   E. Stenius, *Wittgenstein's 'Tractatus'*, Basil Blackwell, 1960, ch.
    XI.
7   P. F. Strawson, *The Bounds of Sense*, Methuen, 1966.

Chapter 6   Sub Specie Aeternitatis I

1   John Hick, 'Religious Faith as Experiencing-As', in *Talk of
    God,* Royal Institute of Philosophy Lectures, 1907–8, p. 33.
    See also *Faith and Knowledge,* Fontana, 1974.
2   John Wisdom, 'Eternal Life', in *Talk of God*, Royal Institute of
    Philosophy Lectures, 1967–8, see particularly pp. 242 ff.
3   Spinoza, *Ethics*, part V, prop. XXX., proof, Everyman
    edition, trans. A. Boyle, J. M. Dent, 1959, pp. 216–17.
4   Wisdom, 'Eternal Life', pp. 245–6, from William James, *The
    Varieties of Religious Experience*, Fontana, 1960, p. 385.
5   Iris Murdoch, *The Sovereignty of Good*, Routledge, 1970, p. 55.

Chapter 7   Sub Specie Aeternitatis II

1   *Critique of Pure Reason*, B672, p. 533.
2   L. Wittgenstein, *Tractatus Logico-Philosophicus*, Routledge,
    1961.
3   I have discussed two of these examples in the following papers:
    'Atheism, Hatred and the Love of God in *The End of the Affair*',
    in *King's Theological Review*, 1978, and 'Saintliness and Sanity'
    in the *Scottish Journal of Religious Studies*, 1980.

Chapter 8   Jesus, the Eternal and Transcendence

1   D. Bonhoeffer, *Letters and Papers from Prison*, SCM Press,
    1973.

2 D. Bonhoeffer, *Christology*, trans. John Bowden, Collins, 1966.
3 *The Sovereignty of Good*, ch. 3.
4 This chapter reproduces a number of paragraphs from my paper 'Ethics and Transcendence in Bonhoeffer', published in the *Scottish Journal of Theology*, 1977.

Chapter 9 History and Faith

1 Van A. Harvey, *The Historian and the Believer*, SCM Press, 1967, pp. 14–15.
2 James Barr, *Old and New in Interpretation*, SCM Press, 1966, p. 67.
3 Denis Nineham in *Christian Believing*, Doctrine Commission of the Church of England, SPCK, 1976, p. 79.
4 M. F. Wiles, *The Remaking of Christian Doctrine*, SCM Press, 1974, p. 45.
5 S. Kierkegaard, *Concluding Unscientific Postscript*, trans. D.F. Swenson and W. Lowrie, Princeton University Press, 1941, p. 25.
6 *Systematic Theology* II, Nisbet, 1957, p. 130.
7 P. Van Buren, *The Secular Meaning of the Gospel*, SCM Press, 1963, pp. 124–5.
8 Nineham, *Christian Believing*, p. 78.
9 Ernst Fuchs, 'The New Testament and the Hermeneutical Problem', in James M. Robinson and John B. Cobb, Jr, (eds), *The New Hermeneutic*, Harper and Row, 1964, p. 114.
10 Schubert M. Ogden, *The Point of Christology*, SCM Press, 1982, p. 15.
11 This chapter reproduces a number of paragraphs from my paper, 'History and Belief', published in *Theology*, January 1970.

Chapter 10 Goodness Incarnate?

1 *Summa Contra Gentiles*, IV, 49.11, University of Notre Dame Press, 1975, p. 210.
2 Dostoevsky, *The Idiot*, Penguin Classics, trans. D. Magarshack, 1955, p. 28.

3 J. Coulson (ed.), *Dostoevsky: A Self-Portrait*, Oxford University Press, 1962, letter 105, p. 168.

4 E. C. Mayne (ed.), *Letters of Dostoevsky*, McGraw-Hill, 1964, p. 142.

5 Eliseo Vivas, 'The Two Dimensions of Reality in *The Brothers Karamazov*', in R. Wellek (ed.), *Dostoevsky*, Prentice-Hall, 1962, pp. 71 ff.

6 See Wellek, *Dostoevsky*, p. 41.

7 *The Idiot*, p. 657.

8 K. Mochulsky, *Dostoevsky*, Princeton University Press, 1967, p. 346.

9 Coulson, *Dostoevsky*, letter 142, p. 224.

10 *Concluding Unscientific Postscript*, p. 175.

11 *Christology*, p. 112.

12 This chapter is adapted from my Inaugural Lecture, delivered in and published by King's College, University of London, in 1978.

Chapter 11 Is Jesus Unique?

1 Harvey, *The Historian and the Believer*, pp. 14–15.

2 Mayor, Fowler and Conway, *Virgil's Messianic Ecloque*, John Murray, 1907, p. 3.

3 Alan Richardson, *The Miracle-Stories of the Gospels*, SCM Press, 1942.

4 I. Kant, *Religion Within the Limits of Reason Alone*, trans. Greene and Hudson, Harper Torchbook, 1960, p. 55.

5 S. Kierkegaard, *Philosophical Fragments*, Princeton University Press, 1962, p. 13.

Chapter 12 Grounds for Optimism?

1 Gabriel Marcel, 'Sketch of a Phenomenology and a Metaphysic of Hope', in *Homo Viator*, Gollancz, 1951, both quotations from p. 34.

2 John Hick, *Death and Eternal Life*, Collins, 1976.

3 See 'Immortality and Resurrection', *Religious Studies* 1967, reprinted in J. Donnelly (ed.), *Language, Metaphysics and Death*, Fordham University Press, 1978, and 'What Happens after

Death?', *Scottish Journal of Theology*, 1969.
4 *The Historian and the Believer*, pp. 280–1.
5 *Concluding Unscientific Postscript*, p. 367.
6 Significant sections of this chapter are drawn from my paper 'Optimism and Pessimism', published in *Religious Studies*, Dec. 1981.

Chapter 13   The Legacy of Theism

1 *Concluding Unscientific Postscript*, p. 223.
2 I have discussed this in my paper 'Immortality and Resurrection'.
3 John Hick (ed.), *The Myth of God Incarnate*, SCM Press, 1977.

Index